The Red and The Blue

The Red and The Blue

Cambridge, Treason and Intelligence

ANDREW SINCLAIR

LITTLE, BROWN AND COMPANY   Boston   Toronto

FIRST AMERICAN EDITION

Library of Congress Cataloging-in-Publication Data
Sinclair, Andrew.
  The red and the blue.
   1. Spies — Great Britain — Biography. 2. Espionage, Russian
— Great Britain. 3. University of Cambridge — Biography.
4. University of Cambridge — History — 20th century. 5. Blunt,
Anthony, 1907–1983. 6. Philby, Kim, 1912–   . 7. Burgess,
Guy, 1911–1963. 8. Maclean, Donald, 1913–   . I. Title.
DA585.A1S56 1986   327.1'2'0922   86–15334
ISBN 0–316–79237–3

RRD VA

PRINTED IN THE UNITED STATES OF AMERICA

To Cambridge, right and wrong

Contents

BOSOLA: It seems you would create me
One of your familiars.
FERDINAND, DUKE OF CALABRIA: Familiar! What's
that?
BOSOLA: Why, a very quaint invisible devil in the flesh,
An intelligencer.

John Webster, *The Duchess of Malfi*

SIR NICHOLAS GIMCRACK: I seldom bring anything
to use; it is not my way. Knowledge is my ultimate end.

Thomas Shadwell, *The Virtuoso*

Introduction to Intelligence

One month before the Central Intelligence Agency was established in 1947, some American scientists disconcerted the Secretary of Defense, James Forrestal. They proved that other scientists might discover the state of national atomic research by reading *Scientific American* and other publications. They could reach the same conclusions on Russian atomic research by reading Soviet publications. Their testimony was used by the defence lawyers of the atomic spy, Klaus Fuchs, to demonstrate that he had merely supplied the Russians with information which was available in scholarly works. Universities could openly provide information that covert operations acquired only by stealth.

Secret intelligence, the British historian Hugh Trevor-Roper has written, should be the continuation of open intelligence by other means. It is particularly so in the world of science. The broadcasting of new discoveries has been desired by most scientists and has proved impossible to prevent for long. The tradition of the open exchange of the results of pure research between leaders in the field is as old as the classical world of the Greeks. The European nations, above all, have created global trade by the export of their technological innovations. While a closed empire like China might try to restrict the knowledge of the manufacture of silk for economic reasons, it could not do so for ever. Silkworms were smuggled out to the west in a hollow tube, one of the first acts of scientific espionage since Prometheus stole fire from the gods. Secrecy is not possible indefinitely in research or industry. There can only be delay in the spread of intelligence.

Intelligence itself is first a capacity and quality of mind: as we

I

say, someone has intelligence or has not; we know that many intelligent people are connected with universities. Intelligence is also a condition of knowledge. What intelligence, for instance, have we about the Russian navy? In a more technical sense, intelligence is an organization and a system, such as British intelligence. And finally, it is a method of processing information, generally available or clandestine, so that an intelligence report may be given to a politician for action. The confusion between intelligent people, the acquisition of intelligence by fair or foul means, the organization of an intelligence service, and the distillation of intelligence for political or economic use is the quagmire where the intelligent sink and treason festers.

At Cambridge, where the world split in two in 1932 or thereabouts with the discovery of atomic fission, there were also separations in traditions of intelligence and within the intelligentsia. By custom, since the founding of the university in the Middle Ages, wandering scholars had come and gone before the age of passport or nation. The disintegrating discoveries of a Newton or a Cavendish were not restricted, but spread abroad. There was no lock on knowledge. The search was for the key to open knowledge to all. Until the nineteenth century, there was no division in Cambridge between the 'two cultures' of the sciences and the arts, later publicized by the first major Cambridge novelist who was also a chemist, C.P.Snow. The dominance, however, of the Church of England at the university did mean that rationalists, atheists and scientific inquirers often failed to win promotion and preferment.

In fact, the first secret societies at Cambridge were opposed to the royal head of the Anglican faith and the church. The Catholic Jacobites of the eighteenth century and the Jacobins after the French Revolution opposed the religious establishment at the university and in London. They were the forerunners of the Conversazione Society, later known as the Apostles, a self-electing élite of those who considered themselves the brightest and the best in contemporary literature and philosophy. The radicals among the Apostles were called Jacobinicals and supported the Spanish liberals in their insurrections in Spain in the 1830s, as they were to do a century further on. In 1848, an Irish Apostle and Member of Parliament,

Smith O'Brien, led a rebellion in Ireland and was sentenced to be hanged, drawn and quartered. Legal Apostolic influence led to his transportation to Australia and eventual pardon, but he showed the usual Apostolic arrogance when he was accused of speaking treason in favour of an Irish Republic in the House of Commons. 'If that be treason,' he declared, 'then I avow treason.'

The split between the openly dominant Anglicans at the university and the clandestine rationalists and radicals was a split of cultures, as was the growing divide between those who practised science or the arts. The industrial revolution had a paradoxical effect on university attitudes. Engineering and applied science furthered the technology which was producing great wealth for the manufacturers, who often exploited their workers and certainly fouled the face of England. Although pure science and mathematics were not directly responsible for the machines derived from their inventions, they seemed to be the Lucifers from whose ideas the new urban Pandaemoniums were developing. The arts, however, could utilize the capital and the benefits of the industrial revolution while decrying its effects. While the fellow of a college in the Georgian age could hope to keep up with discoveries in all fields, the specialization demanded by the Victorians and the products of that specialization divided the Cambridge intelligentsia. There were no scientists, for instance, elected to the Apostles during the whole nineteenth century, and only four before the Second World War, although some mathematicians were favoured by the society because of their long correspondence with philosophers.

The growing differences between the scientific and the literary élite, between the tradition of the open exchange of knowledge and the secret associations necessary to radical cliques, were exaggerated by the classical inheritance of so many of the arts fellows of the Cambridge colleges. The ideal of the bachelor don giving his time and feelings to young students, already conditioned towards male love by the ancient Greek teaching in the leading public schools, was, by its very nature, a thing of the shadows, for English society prosecuted homosexuals legally and preached the early Roman virtues of clear thinking and clean living, *mens sana in corpore sano*, to the dominant Anglicans at the university, who tried to make

3

sure that the battle for young minds and bodies would be won in the chapels and on the playing-fields of Cambridge rather than in the hidden tea-rooms of those colleges of Old Etonians and the Apostles, King's and Trinity. It was no accident that the coded Victorian poem, *In Memoriam*, was written by the Apostles' greatest poet, Alfred Lord Tennyson, to a beloved brother in the society, Arthur Hallam, upon his early death. It was no coincidence that the Apostle and Fellow of King's, William Johnson Cory, the author of the Eton Boating Song and the translator of Callimachus's famous epitaph to Heraclitus, had to resign his teaching post after being involved in a homosexual scandal with the Earl of Rosebery. The wits among the Apostles had their term for their version of Platonic love – the Higher Sodomy.

Two other chords, major and minor, struck a dissonance within Cambridge society. Between wars, nationalism was rarely popular among the leading intellectuals. When the trumpets sounded, however, the dash of the best minds to the defence of the red, white and blue exceeded the Charge of the Light Brigade and approached the death wish of lemmings. When Britain was not fighting her enemies, patriotism was discounted, peace and international good feelings were valued. The university nurtured confident radicals like Lord Byron well before the Communist traitors of the nineteen-thirties. It was only when the clouds of conflict gathered that nearly all the best minds found themselves engaged in defending the realm. Opposition to war had to go underground. Open pacifism, as Bertrand Russell proved in the First World War, could lead to expulsion from a college lectureship.

The subversion of the Anglican establishment, the opposition to the social changes caused by the scientific and industrial revolutions, the classical heritage and the sexual preferences of a closed male society, a sense of aristocratic superiority unbound by custom or law, these all furthered the minor Cambridge tradition of clandestine association practised by the Apostles, who tried to prefer themselves through their group because the state and the university might not. Above all, they stood against the establishment and the Church of England. Every college had its own chapel, and there were more churches to the square mile in Cambridge than anywhere north secrets demanded for the service of Russian society were often used for its military machine. More important to the Kremlin than its few agents among the Apostles were the scientists who met in Trinity at the Kapitsa Club, weekly and openly, to discuss with the Russian physicist Peter Kapitsa the latest discoveries in their fields of research. Kapitsa, who spent thirteen years at the Cavendish during its golden age, took back with him to Russia after 1934 not only the secrets of the atom and fission research, but the contents of his Cambridge laboratory. He also kept the confidence of almost all the leading physicists in the western world, who continued to exchange with him all the scientific information that their governments did not embargo.

To wish to change domestic or international society in the thirties did not involve being an Apostle or serving as a foreign agent. More effective was to be asked to join the Tots and Quots, a weekly London dining-club of radical scientists and economists, who might be expected to play a part in the actual transformation of the condition of man. They were characterized during a debate in the House of Lords, which many of them were eventually to join, as a group of young men from the universities, 'destined for eminence in the scientific world and, all of them, for key positions as the "tame magicians" of the war.' Among them were Solly Zuckerman and Hyman Levy, Desmond Bernal and Jack Haldane, Lancelot Hogben and Joseph Needham, while the economists included Hugh Gaitskell and Roy Harrod. Members of the club, in an influential paperback called *Science in War*, not only prodded the government into recruiting themselves and their colleagues into service, but drew up for the post-war Labour government a memorandum on a Government Science Secretariat that made Britain follow Russia in the funding and use of its best scientific minds to better the conditions of its society, industry and defence.

With the coming of the nuclear age, governments learned to harness science and technology to national needs, in time of peace as well as in time of conflict. In that respect, they were one world war behind the Russians. Scientific information began to be treated in the same way as political information. The importance of it was recognized, although chiefly in military matters, particularly in the discoveries of the atomic spies. Although economics was becoming more significant than politics in the management of countries, industrial or scientific espionage was punished lightly compared with the betrayal of political intelligence. While minor agents such as Vassall briefly became household names and served long prison sentences, hundreds of technological spies were undetected or reprimanded without court action. Yet the growing interpenetration of economics and scientific research and defence planning, which the American President Dwight Eisenhower termed the military-industrial complex, led to the conclusion that all discoveries that might benefit a nation's trade or defence became matters of security. Intelligence was no longer a quality of mind to be shared openly with everybody. It was knowledge to be protected or acquired by any appropriate method and by any organization designated by a state or multinational company. The processing of that intelligence became the support of all governments that were addicted to its use.

No longer could a scientist disclose his research without being aware of his responsibility for its application. No more could the free exchange of information excuse the revelation of so-called national secrets. In the country of the gagged, the close-mouthed man is king.

1 Fallen Leaves

'As the generations of leaves,' Glaucus told Diomedes in the *Iliad*, 'so are the generations of men.' The siege of Troy was the Great War of Grecian myth, when the aristocrats of Hellas were cut down. An echo of Homer's sentence was sounded in Trinity chapel at Cambridge, when the sermon on Remembrance Day every November began: 'It is the time of fallen leaves.' The Reverend Mr Simpson was mourning his dead friends, the lost generation of young men killed in another Great War, the First World War, the war to end all wars that only led to another world war. All the bravest and the best had gone according to his lament, among them the poet Rupert Brooke. The twenty-one years of peace between the two World Wars was an uneasy truce of disillusionment; the surviving governors were old men or mediocre young men risen in the absence of the glorious dead. 'Since then, small men have made shift to fill great places.'

Cambridge had reason to remember the First World War. To fight in it as an officer meant probable death, mutilation or injury. Of those who graduated in the five years before the outbreak of the war, more than a quarter were killed, more than a half wounded. The slaughter was the massacre of a class that expected to rule. At one time in the war, the survival time of a second lieutenant in the front line was estimated at six weeks. He was meant to lead over the top, reconnoitre between the trenches at night, bring in the casualties from the barbed wire and expose himself first to every risk. Small wonder that he died at three times the rate of his soldiers. A privilege in birth and education seemed a privilege in death and extinction. 'Our generation becomes history,' Duff Cooper wrote to Lady Diana Manners in 1918, 'instead of growing up.'

Those, like Bertrand Russell, who had avoided fighting were convinced of the virtue of their pacifism. They had survived; many
of their friends had not. Better to be a live lord, Duff Cooper wrote,
than a dead lieutenant. The ending of the war brought the loss
home. There would be no replacement of those who had gone. 'One
will at last fully recognise', Lady Cynthia Asquith wrote in her
diary, 'that the dead are not only dead for the duration of the war.'
The young 'Souls' from Oxford were nearly all fallen, Raymond
Asquith and Aubrey Herbert and the Grenfell brothers, as were
some of the young members of the Cambridge Apostles. The walls
of the quadrangles of the Oxbridge colleges were covered with the
lists of the honoured dead: at Eton, still the breeding ground of
Conservative ministers, 1,150 Old Etonians were commemorated,
one killed in five of those who had served in uniform. Not since
the Napoleonic Wars a century before had there been such a decimation of fighting men and future leaders. It had also been the first
war of mass conscription in England, where only the few had refused
to serve. Some of these came from Cambridge, more from the artistic
group given the name of the London district of Bloomsbury, which
was to rise to undue influence through its attitude to the war and
the thinning of the ranks of its cultural competitors in the trenches.
Those who did not fight stayed alive and had the last words. Those
who did survive often felt guilty. 'Nobody, nothing, will shift me
from the belief, which I shall take to the grave,' wrote J.B.Priestley,
a lieutenant in the war, later an undergraduate at Trinity Hall,
Cambridge, 'that the generation to which I belong, destroyed
between 1914 and 1918, was a great generation, marvellous in its
promise. This is not self-praise, because those of us who are left
know that we are the runts.'

The legend of the lost generation was, numerically, only a legend.
A generation may be a group of much the same age existing at
the same time from the same country and involved in the same
fate. Of course, that group is split by considerations of class, income,
education, sex, religion and heritage. But when a country is led
by an élite, as England still was after the Armistice and the Peace
of Versailles, that élite seems to itself to be the important generation

within a generation. Its survivors had almost a sense of guilt about their existence. They exaggerated the numbers and the quality of the dead. Future Prime Ministers lived, such as the badly-wounded Harold Macmillan and Anthony Eden. It was untrue that the bravest and best had been extirpated. The methods of killing by artillery bombardment, machine-gun fire, mine, bomb and gas were random. There was little discrimination by character in that wayward slaughter. Statistically, 700,000 British combatants died, of which 37,500 were officers, a proportion of some nineteen to one. There had been five million British males between the ages of twenty and forty before the Great War, but there was the same number alive three years after the end of the war. A generation had certainly not been killed: some of its more brilliant members had, while others had suffered terribly.

The myth of the missing generation grew not because of the horrors of the war, but because of the disillusion of the peace. John Maynard Keynes, a leading Apostle and member of the Bloomsbury group, had been the chief representative of the British Treasury at the post-war negotiations in Paris, and he denounced the terms reached at Versailles in a polemic called *The Economic Consequences of the Peace*. It condemned the punitive reparations exacted from Germany and the self-interested land exchanges of the victorious powers. He foresaw that the consequences of the peace would be the financial ruin of Europe and another world war. 'Vengeance', he predicted, 'will not limp.' Nothing would delay a final civil war between the forces of reaction and revolution. In that conflict, the horrors of the late German war would fade into nothing. It would destroy 'whoever is the victor, the civilisation and the progress of our generation'.

This was to become the governing attitude of many of the leading intellectuals at Cambridge and in London. Members of the generation of 1914 that had gone to war so readily were discomfited by the peace. Their feeling of betrayal by the old men governing them had led to revolutions in Europe, suppressed outside Soviet Russia, and to the rise of Fascist movements, particularly in Italy. Extreme solutions advocating social change of the left or of the right promised a catharsis as violent as the recent European conflict,

itself welcomed originally by a host of young men as an answer
to the political turmoil of the pre-war years. The myth of the lost
generation produced in its survivors revulsion and a determination
never to repeat the horrors of the slaughter. Its legacy was a certain
pacifism that would culminate in the notorious Oxford Union resolution of 1933, when the House carried a motion refusing to fight
for King and Country; radical political and economic solutions
to society's problems that would push Sir Oswald Mosley towards
Fascism and the late Lord Milford towards Communism; and a
disdain for the establishment that influenced the Bright Young
Thinkers against the conventions of their time.

There were notorious pacifists and radicals among the Apostles
at Cambridge, and among the Bloomsbury group that was so much
a creation of the Apostles. The object of the society was to put
all in question, what one member Donald MacAlister in 1908 called
'the ethereal atmosphere of free and audacious inquiry'. It was
an élite of the male élite which swore its members not only to
secrecy, but encouraged them to seek only one another's exclusive
company. They were the best minds engaging in the pursuit of
truth and beauty, although, as Virginia Woolf remarked, they
often had no physical splendour themselves. They were divorced
from any concern for king, country or material wealth. They were
a conspiracy of the self-elected, answerable only to one another.
Each member, MacAlister declared of the absent Angels and Apostles, was with the society at every private meeting on Saturday
evenings at King's. 'There he mastered the art of reconciling by
a phrase the most divergent of hypotheses, the most fundamentally
antagonistic of antinomies. There he grew accustomed to differ from
his comrades in nothing but opinion.... Towards midnight on a
Saturday, he too would soar. Others might find the medium but
a vacuum.... But *he* was no chimaera, for he felt his reality and
knew that he was alive.' The world of Reality, indeed, was contained
within the society. The rest of the world was merely an Appearance.

This secret society with latter-day Platonic pretensions based at
King's did contain many of the best minds of the age: Bertrand
Russell and John Maynard Keynes, G.E. Moore and Ludwig Witt-
genstein, E.M. Forster and G.M. Trevelyan, Desmond MacCarthy

and Edward Marsh (later Sir Winston Churchill's private secretary), the Lucases and Stracheys, and many more. Most were concerned with the arts, a few were economists or mathematicians such as Keynes and G.H.Hardy, hardly one was in the sciences, which were held to deal with formulae rather than syllogisms. Most of the Apostles, indeed, would have shared Flaubert's pet hates – railways, factories and chemists – which gave the illusion of human progress through scientific advance, not through moral progress. The leading Apostolic philosopher, G.E.Moore, dominated the thinking of the society and its disciples with his *Principia Ethica*, a book more honoured in its misunderstanding than its observance. As Keynes declared to Lytton Strachey, it ruled the Apostles' way of thinking and everything else. 'How amazing to think that only we know the rudiments of a true theory of ethic.' It was the revelation of right conduct to the chosen few.

Moore himself replaced the Idealistic schools of philosophical thought prevalent among the Apostles with a literal and personal examination of things. His assertions became questions to others: 'What exactly do you mean?' His favourite quotation was Bishop Butler's statement: 'Everything is what it is and not another thing.' He was held to destroy Victorian values by asserting that acting in pursuit of pleasure and self-improvement benefited the general good. People should not do things to help one another, but to help themselves. Enlightened self-interest led to the benefit of all. Keynes admitted that the Apostles took from Moore his religion, so to speak, and discarded his morals, which were still utilitarian. 'One of the greatest advantages of his religion was that it made morals unnecessary – meaning by "religion" one's attitude to oneself and the ultimate and by "morals" one's attitude towards the outside world.... Nothing mattered except states of mind, chiefly our own.'

The disciples of the *Principia Ethica* felt free to follow 'love, the creation and enjoyment of aesthetic experience and the pursuit of knowledge. Of these love came a long way first.' This concentration on love led to the later notoriety of the Apostles and their offshoot, the Bloomsbury group. The homosexual loves of many of the Apostles and the complicated bisexual catch-as-catch-can of many of the Bloomsberries shocked and fascinated later generations. 'We repudiated entirely customary morals, conventions and traditional wisdom,' Keynes concluded. 'We were, that is to say, in the strict sense of the term, immoralists. The consequences of being found out had, of course, to be considered for what they were worth. But we recognized no moral obligation on us, no inner sanction, to conform or obey.'

Bertrand Russell thought that Keynes and Lytton Strachey and other Apostles and Bloomsberries made Moore responsible for their own version of the good life, which was the passionate mutual admiration of a clique of the élite. Moore was a moralist and not responsible for his followers, any more than Freud was for the Freudians or Marx for the Marxists. Some of the Apostles and Bloomsberries were moralists and proud of it: these were people of strong individual opinions, with only a tendency of thought in common. But that tendency was generally in favour of a personal liberation in pursuit of beauty, love and truth. It was a combination of a pacific method and a revolutionary purpose. After Moore, an Apostle and a Bloomsberry was capable of any thought or action within his or her religion of self. The poet Roy Campbell summed up this narcissistic feeling in his 'Home Thoughts on Bloomsbury':

> Of all the clever people round me here
> I most delight in me –
> Mine is the only voice I hear
> And mine the only face I see.

The links between the Apostles and the Bloomsbury group were close. The two daughters of the leading Cambridge man of letters, Leslie Stephen, went after his death to live at 46 Gordon Square in Bloomsbury. Their brother Thoby, soon himself to die, brought many of his Apostolic friends from Cambridge to visit his sisters, Virginia and Vanessa, of whom the latter was to marry Clive Bell from Trinity. 'You could say what you liked about art, sex, or religion,' Vanessa Bell testified. 'Life was exciting, terrible and amusing and one had to explore it thankful that one could do so freely.' Her son Quentin listed twenty members of the Bloomsbury group in 1913, of whom ten were Apostles and fourteen had been either to King's or Trinity, Cambridge. The leaders of the group were

usually Apostles, such as Leonard Woolf, who married Virginia
Stephen; Lytton and James Strachey; Maynard Keynes and E.M.
Forster; Bertrand Russell was not considered really a Bloomsberry,
although he often visited them. All knew one another well, particularly Maynard Keynes and Lytton Strachey from their earlier days
at Cambridge and in the Apostles. Strachey once wrote an inspired
piece of doggerel about his friend, which summed up many of the
admired traits of those in the Society. Keynes was:

> Both penetrating and polite
> A liberal and a sodomite,
> An atheist and a statistician,
> A man of sense, without ambition.
> A man of business, without bustle,
> A follower of Moore and Russell,
> One who, in fact, in every way
> Combined the features of the day.

The element of homosexuality among the Apostles and the
Bloomsbury group was the taboo of the old regime. However prevalent in London and at Cambridge, it was considered a vice and
had disgraced many, such as Lord Arthur Somerset and Oscar
Wilde. Although romantic friendships between young men were
praised in Greek literature and normal in the public schools,
although Socrates's love of Alcibiades was an inspiration to many
of the Apostles who loved youthful male beauty, the subject and
the practice were rarely brought out into the open before the revolt
against customary values of the Apostles and the Bloomsberries.
It was after an all-male Founder's Feast at King's in 1909, that
Maynard Keynes wrote to Duncan Grant, declaring the evening
to be the mark of an epoch in the history of the college's manners.
Previously, if there was debauchery, it was private. 'Quite suddenly
our rigid rules of convention that one kisses no one in public utterly
collapsed – and we all kissed! The scene really can't be described....
Everybody was there. What our reppers will be, heaven knows.'

Open demonstrations were rare, but the praise and practice of
male affection were not. As Moore might have phrased it, some
Cambridge homosexuals were Apostles. Many Apostles were overt

or covert homosexuals. Some Apostles were also Bloomsberries. Not all Apostles or Bloomsberries were homosexuals. But certainly to them homosexual behaviour between consenting adults was no vice. Vicious was the death of beautiful young men like Rupert Brooke in an unnecessary carnage.

The attitude of most members of Bloomsbury and the Apostles to the war was to become significant in the peace. Cambridge as a whole was patriotic enough. There was quite a stampede to duty. As the pacific Apostle Lowes Dickinson noted:

> The younger dons and even the older ones disappeared into war work. All discussion, all pursuit of truth ceased as in a moment. To win the war or to hide safely among the winners became the only preoccupation. Abroad was heard only the sound of the guns, at home only the ceaseless patter of a propaganda utterly indifferent to truth.

Among the Apostles, two of the younger members were to die, the poet Rupert Brooke of blood-poisoning off Skyros (his younger brother Alfred was killed in France) and Ferenc Békássy, a Hungarian aristocrat, who fought for his own country and paid the price, although his fellow countryman and Apostle, the philosopher Ludwig Wittgenstein, survived the butchery as an Austrian officer on the Russian front. As a Trinity undergraduate before the war, Wittgenstein had asked Bertrand Russell, 'Do you think I am an absolute idiot?' If he was, he would become an aeronaut; if he was not, he would become a philosopher. His major work, the *Tractatus Logico-Philosophicus*, was written in the trenches, and the manuscript survived the fighting and Russell's criticisms to become as important as the *Principia Ethica*, with its rigorous methods of asking questions and examining meaningful statements.

The First World War divided even the community of the Apostles and set them at one another's throats. Other fellows from King's co-operated in inventing the tank and the military bridge, and particularly in deciphering German messages in Room 40 of the Admiralty under Sir Alfred Ewing, who recruited the best minds from his old college to assess the positions of the German fleet and its submarines. The battles of the Dogger Bank and Jutland were predicted on the banks of the Cam.

A few protested against the war; the most famous of them were Bertrand Russell and Lytton Strachey. Russell found his life before and after 1914 to be like Faust's life before and after he met Mephistopheles. He wrote pacifist pamphlets and was convicted under the Defence of the Realm Act, later serving six months in Brixton prison. He was denied a fellowship at Trinity and deprived of his college lectureship; he commented that the younger fellows of Trinity were serving as army officers, so that the older fellows all wanted to do their bit by punishing him. In a celebrated answer to the question frequently put to conscientious objectors, 'What would you do if a German officer tried to rape your sister?', Lytton Strachey replied: 'I should try to get between them.' He and Clive Bell and Duncan Grant were pacifists, while Leonard Woolf was rejected by a medical board and studied international peace settlements. Keynes shared the views of his Bloomsbury friends, but continued to do war work in the Treasury, trying to preserve the value of the pound. 'I work for a Government I despise,' he wrote after peace proposals had been rejected in 1917, 'for ends I think criminal.'

The war was to be ignored until it was safe to resist it. The thing was to survive out of the reach of conscription. The belligerent writer Percy Wyndham Lewis attacked the Bloomsberries for 'all doing war-work of "National Importance" down in some downy English county, under the wings of powerful pacifist friends: pruning trees, planting gooseberry bushes, and haymaking, doubtless in large sunbonnets.' D.H.Lawrence, himself ambivalent about the war, blamed them for their irreverent assault on all values: he dreamt of them as stinging beetles and had a horror of their little swarming selves. Lytton Strachey's scandalous success of 1918, however, his biography of *Eminent Victorians*, was such an assault on heroic reputations as well as Victorian beliefs that Bloomsbury's own opinions about the values of the past and the armed struggle finally began to seem both important and relevant.

It was a revolt of a small group of privileged people with private incomes, who felt divorced from political considerations, except for Maynard Keynes and Leonard Woolf. In fact, Vanessa Bell was notorious for sitting next to H.H.Asquith at dinner and asking him whether he was interested in politics: he was actually the Prime Minister. The Bloomsberries changed artistic taste: two Post-Impressionist exhibitions sponsored by Roger Fry and Clive Bell made the London world redefine its perceptions in the images of Gauguin and Van Gogh and Cézanne, Picasso and Matisse. E.M.Forster, their major novelist until the later writings of Virginia Woolf, attacked his country's beliefs about the virtues of public schools and imperialism, of liberalism and fair business dealings. Many of the country's literary pages were controlled at times by friends. Leonard Woolf was at the *Nation*, Desmond MacCarthy was at the *New Statesman*, and Lytton Strachey's uncle ran the *Spectator*. Reviews of Apostolic works were assured. The opinions of Bloomsbury were printed and circulated.

By the last year of trench warfare, there was a widespread disillusion with the generals in command and with the foul methods of fighting, a stalemate in the mud which resulted in millions of deaths, made more horrible by the outbreak of an epidemic of influenza that also killed civilians in their millions. Heroism was, in Quentin Bell's words, at a discount. It had been highly valued, then inflated, and was now devalued. A certain scepticism, uneasiness and disenchantment replaced the glorious certainties of 1914, 'and in that mood the British public was ready to listen to what Bloomsbury had to say', particularly about the waste of the war.

The profound emotional impact of the horror and slaughter – Noel Annan believed – convinced many that previous values were wrong and perhaps responsible for the catastrophe. The Bloomsbury group with its Apostolic advisers 'produced that violent change in the code of behaviour which severed the twenties from the *Ancien Régime*'. More important than the Socialist code of conduct suggested by the Fabians and the Webbs was the growth of the private virtues suggested by Moore and Virginia Woolf, a reaction from the collective madness of the world war.

Bertrand Russell himself seemed to reflect both the futility of most of the Apostles and the Bloomsbury group during the fighting, and also the changes that the experience of the conflict had made in their attitudes.

> When the War was over [Russell confessed], I saw that all I had done had been totally useless except to myself. I had not saved a single life or shortened the War by a minute. I had not succeeded in doing anything to diminish the bitterness which caused the Treaty of Versailles. But at any rate I had not been an accomplice in the crime of all the belligerent nations, and for myself I had acquired a new philosophy and a new youth. I had got rid of the don and the Puritan. I had learned an understanding of instinctive processes which I had not possessed before, and I had acquired a certain poise from having stood so long alone.

Part of another élite had been destroyed in the fighting, hardly mentioned beside the lost 'Souls' and Apostles and other famed young men from the ruling class. That was the scientific élite. One member was Henry Moseley, killed at the Dardanelles, the apple of Sir Ernest Rutherford's eye at the Cavendish Laboratory, where he was conducting research into atomic physics. Rutherford wrote:

> It was a national tragedy that our military organization at the start was so inelastic as to be unable, with a few exceptions, to utilize the offers of services of our scientific men except as combatants in the firing line. Our regret for the untimely end of Moseley is all the more poignant that we cannot but recognize that his services would have been far more useful to his country in one of the numerous fields of scientific inquiry rendered necessary by the war than by exposure to the chances of a Turkish bullet.

Science was not yet valued as a major instrument of war. When the United States first became a belligerent, some officials of the American Chemical Society offered the services of their members to the War Department. Their offer was refused with the words, 'We already have a chemist.' So much for scientists in action, although it was a war in which technology and chemistry were already playing a great role, in submarine and air warfare, in tank and gas attacks. Certainly in England, powerful figures such as

Henry Tizard and F.A.Lindemann were establishing themselves as scientific advisers to governments: Lindemann himself had to learn to fly at the Royal Aircraft Factory at Farnborough to prove his algebraic formula for getting out of spinning nose-dives without crashing. The contribution of scientists to the war effort was immense: their discoveries did much to break the stalemate in military thinking that bogged the fighting down in trenches and on oceans.

There was hardly a scientist among the Apostles and none in the Bloomsbury group, of which only three ever held academic jobs. Their eminence outside the arts lay in economics through Maynard Keynes and philosophy through Moore, Russell and Wittgenstein. When Quentin Bell was mocking the influence of the group, he could allege that, because of Keynes's influence, we still live in an era of Bloomsbury capitalism regulated by Bloomsbury banking and Bloomsbury tax structures. There is an element of truth in that, because the Bloomsbury group was opposed to Marxism and Fascism and the state direction of the economy: it believed in the use of inherited capital and private incomes to subsidize the good life of the privileged few. Keynes himself in *The Economic Consequences of the Peace* had predicted the coming collapse of the European economy; he was to become the saviour of capitalism through those doctrines of deficit spending known as Keynesianism. In so far as he wished to protect the way of life of his chosen group of friends by his policies, Keynes was the financier of the Bloomsberries just as he was the financier of King's through his advice on the college's investments.

The Apostles secretly and the Bloomsbury group openly were cultural and sexual rebels. They were élitists whose views influenced an élite. They had no direct mass appeal, and little power outside London. Even in post-war Oxford and Cambridge, their influence was restricted to the intellectual leaders in the arts. During the twenties, most of the undergraduates worked for their degrees and took little notice of the attitudes of Bloomsbury. The preaching of personal values and disillusion with the post-war world was slow to spread down from the top. It would take the great depression and the rise of Fascism to radicalize many of the young, who would then exploit the attack on Victorian and Edwardian values pioneered by the Apostles and the Bloomsbury group.

The later leader of the British Fascist movement, Sir Oswald Mosley, had served in the war and had decided not to go to Oxford or Cambridge. His contemporaries there did not seem to know much that he did not. The war was the vital experience, the peace was the disillusion, the old values and the old men who had failed in both needed replacement.

> Smooth, smug people, who had never fought or suffered [he wrote of Armistice Day celebrations] seemed to the eyes of youth – at that moment age-old with sadness, weariness and bitterness – to be eating, drinking, laughing on the graves of our companions. I stood aside from the delirious throng; silent and alone, ravaged by memory. Driving purpose had begun; there must be no more war. I dedicated myself to politics.

He would declare war himself against the old men, 'who muddled my generation into the crisis of 1914, who muddled us into the crisis of 1931 – the old men who have laid waste the power and the glory of the land'.

The legend of the lost generation sacrificed by the old men who muddled the war and the peace became a cult of the dead that accounted for the failures of the present. The best young minds were said to be killed, although hardly anyone counted the scientists or the future Labour leaders among them. In fact, Clement Attlee survived the fighting, but many other leading young Socialists did not. They were not alive to oppose the false old men with the wrong values. The inadequate were rising to take their places. The Bloomsbury group never recognized that its own pre-eminence and influence had something to do with the lack of surviving competition. And as for the Apostles, most of them lived through a war that disturbed neither their secrecy nor their morals. Only two of the leaves that fell from that generation of young men fell from their privet hedge.

2 Two Cultures

At the end of 1918, after surviving the war, Robert Graves observed that there were two distinct Britains. They were not the two Britains of governing and governed classes, as in pre-war times, but 'the Fighting Forces, meaning literally the soldiers and sailors who had fought... and the Rest, including the Government. They talked such different languages that men home on leave after months on active service felt like visitors to a foreign country.'

Briefly, the returning combatants were treated as heroes, but peacetime had its own forgetfulness for past warriors. Many of the returned university undergraduates were invalids: Graves claimed that anyone who had served in the trenches for five months or had suffered from rolling artillery barrages was ill. 'Shell-shock' afflicted all soldiers, leading to alternate moods of apathy and high excitement, with quick reactions and loss of concentration. Nervous breakdowns and alcoholism were common several years after the war had ended. And these sick men had returned to a peace mismanaged by their Liberal war leader, David Lloyd George, who appeared to be losing most of Ireland in a brutal way, to be handing over Europe to French domination, to be attacking the Russian Revolution with expeditionary forces, and to be encouraging high prices, followed by a slump and unemployment. This was no good land or stable world fit for homecoming heroes.

The rapid gains of the Labour Party at the expense of the Liberals in the post-war years were a measure of the disillusion of the returned combatants, particularly from the intellectual élite. It was noticeable that when the Labour leader Ramsay MacDonald first became Prime Minister in 1924, half the party's Members of Parlia-

ment were from middle-class backgrounds, only half from the working-class or the trade union movement. The Labour Party had little
of the militance of European Socialist organizations. It was a democratic party, above all. It did not subscribe to revolution and the
dictatorship of the proletariat, which meant the dictatorship of a
Politburo. It excluded known Communists from its membership.

The influence and power of the Communist party in England
in the twenties was inconsiderable. A leading Bolshevik and later
Soviet Foreign Minister, Maxim Litvinov, had come to England
in 1919, to recruit leading English intellectuals as founders of a
Communist Party of Great Britain. In the provisional party executive, three of the fourteen members were from the intelligentsia,
while some two-thirds of prominent British Communists or fellow-
travellers in the twenties had graduated from Oxbridge. They
included the Palme Dutt brothers, John Strachey and Raymond
Postgate, Andrew Rothstein and Emile Burns, and the influential
Cambridge economist Maurice Dobb. Their influence in the twenties was important only because of the fear they aroused, not because
of their significance.

'We should distinguish between the object of fear and the cause
of fear,' Wittgenstein points out in his *Philosophical Investigations*.
The cause of fear is often not its cause, but its target. Its existence,
however negligible, makes it the victim of the fears of others. The
British Communist Party and Bolshevik intelligence and propaganda in the twenties were only targets. Yet the fear of them brought
down the first Labour government of Ramsay MacDonald in 1924.
The government had decided not to prosecute the editor of the
Workers' Weekly for an article urging soldiers to drop their weapons
in a class or military war. Its previous allies, the Liberals, joined
the Conservatives in passing a censure motion against the government. Before the next election, the publication of the Zinoviev Letter
– allegedly some instructions from the Third International based
in Moscow to British Communists on the subversion of the state
– seemed to damn the Labour Party as a Communist front. Ramsay
MacDonald had been brilliant in making Labour appear a democratic and rational party, not, as he wrote, 'a "Red Terror" to the
minds of large masses of people who knew little about it'. Now

waving that red flag lost an election.

Engels had once told Marx that the British proletariat was bourgeois, not revolutionary. That was proved by the General Strike of 1926, which began with a protracted miners' strike and was followed by a resolution of the Trades Union Congress to bring out all unionists. The workers' revolution was, however, only a nine days' wonder. Its failure effectively destroyed the idea of the militant overthrow of the government by the proletariat and put the trade union movement into moderate Labour hands for the next forty years.

The reaction to the General Strike at Cambridge showed how bourgeois the undergraduates were and how little sympathy existed for the workers. Over half the undergraduates registered for emergency duty, running communications or delivering food; nearly a third of them acted as strike-breakers and special constables. As one college magazine observed, most of the young men saw the strike as a gigantic rag: even sympathy for Socialism did not survive the lure of driving a train. The dons themselves split two to one against a manifesto urging the government to open negotiations with the Trades Union Congress. At that time, there were only a hundred and fifty members of the university Labour Club, and perhaps thirty Communists in the whole of Cambridge. With the leading economist Maynard Keynes denouncing Marxism as complicated hocus-pocus with only the value of muddle-headedness, the Soviet system had small appeal for the young élite.

Marxism was, however, a materialist faith. The point was to achieve a physical and practical revolution in human society. The Soviet government was as interested in recruiting scientific advisers from abroad as political sympathizers: better if they were both. Even more important than the Apostles in King's College were the researchers in the Cavendish Laboratory. As Marx had declared in his *Theses on Feuerbach*, 'The philosophers have only *interpreted* the world in various ways; the point, however, is to *change* it.'

'If what the Bolsheviks are doing to Russia is an experiment,' the physiologist Ivan Pavlov declared in 1918, 'it is one to which I would not subject even a frog.' At the time, the Imperial Academy

of Sciences in Russia was a small independent body, not subject
to state control; its allied research institutes and academies were
also free. That was to change. Cold and hunger, financial and actual
starvation, killed off the academicians. Within two years, the Director of the Botanical Institute noted that the ranks of Soviet scientists
were getting thinner day by day. In 1921, the secret police killed
off sixty intellectuals, claiming them to be part of the Tagantsev
conspiracy. It was the beginning of a systematic persecution of independent scholars in the Soviet Union. The writer Maxim Gorki's
protests to Lenin fell on deaf ears. Twelve years after the Revolution,
the Academy was purged: one hundred of its employees were
arrested, five hundred were dismissed. Its leading members were
persuaded to support the Bolshevik Party or were forced into retirement or exile: good party members with little scientific knowledge
replaced them in the Academy. Two more show trials in 1929 and
1930 condemned the historian Platonov and the scientist Ramzin
and their colleagues. Large groups of microbiologists were arrested
and forced to work in special institutes such as those at Suzdal
and Lake Seliger; there they manufactured chemical and bacteriolo-
gical weapons. Agricultural experts and botanists and geneticists
were decimated as an explanation of the failure of the Five Year
Plans for collective farming.

Lenin had proclaimed that there could be no impartial social
science in a society founded on class struggle. Scientists were thus
brought under the control of the Kremlin. Their quality was reduced
by the introduction of tens of thousands of ill-trained students and
faithful members of the Party. Military considerations dictated the
application of state funds to scientific research and the appointments
to institutes. Pavlov himself had to accept political domination to
preserve his grants for his experiments and for travel abroad. At
a meeting of the Academy of Sciences he supported the admission
of an old Bolshevik who had never been to college. Caligula had
his horse elected as a Roman consul, Pavlov declared, so why object
to the election of a decent old revolutionary?

With state control of science secured at home, the Kremlin also
looked for contributions from scientists abroad, particularly from
the capitalist countries. Russian scientists, however, had to assist

Socialism at home and hoard their discoveries. A moving plea of a group of Soviet physicists was ignored:

Science is international by its very nature. It represents the results of the collective experience of all humanity, and requires uninterrupted contacts and interchanges between human beings, and in particular the scientists of all countries, so that they can at once make use of one another's discoveries.

For the first four years after the Revolution, scientists were hardly allowed to leave Russia. Then a trade mission led by the mathematician and naval designer Aleksey Krylov was sent in 1921 to buy scientific instruments and supplies in Europe. The group included the physicist Abram Joffé and his brilliant pupil the young Peter Leonidovich Kapitsa. It visited the Cavendish Laboratory at Cambridge, where Sir Ernest (later Lord) Rutherford had assembled a pioneering group of experimental physicists.

There was already an organization sympathetic to Soviet Russia in Britain. The National Union of Scientific Workers had been created after the First World War. It was particularly strong in Cambridge where its branch was strongly supported by the radical mathematician and Apostle, G.H.Hardy. The Marxist economist Maurice Dobb from Pembroke College was admitted and formed a cell within the Union along with other Communists such as Clemens Palme Dutt. He visited Moscow in 1922 with the future leader of the Communist Party of Great Britain, Harry Pollitt. Contacts were made, the uses of British scientific knowledge to the Bolshevik Revolution were explained. Other Communists at Cambridge included the brilliant Jesuit-trained Irish crystallographer and physicist Desmond Bernal, and Roy Pascal, a Marxist fellow of Pembroke College who shared with Dobb a house in Chesterton Lane where sympathizers could meet. These formed the nucleus of the university Communists.

The Russian government also believed in the direct approach. Joffé consulted Rutherford on the state of physics, and permission was requested for Kapitsa to work at the Cavendish as a research assistant, subsidized by the Russian purchasing mission. He was accepted by Rutherford on condition that he did not introduce politics to the study of physics. Marxism-Leninism had nothing to do with scientific research. With Joffé, Kapitsa was to become the father of nuclear research in the Soviet Union and an adviser on the making of the Russian atom and hydrogen bombs. He had chosen to attend or was placed at the Cavendish at the opening of the golden age of experimental physics. Rutherford appreciated Kapitsa's background in engineering. He himself always emphasized the 'turning out of the real solid facts of Nature' rather than the revolutionary theoretical physics of Planck and Einstein, Niels Bohr at Copenhagen, Max Born and Heisenberg at Göttingen, and Louis de Broglie in Paris. While Cambridge only produced one leading theoretical physicist, Paul Dirac, who applied relativity theory to quantum mechanics, the Cavendish developed experimental physics to the point where atomic particles could be disintegrated, their structure changed.

Rutherford and his disciples believed in the open exchange of knowledge, the international role of physics. Scientists who worked under Rutherford came from fourteen countries, including Bulgaria, China, Germany, Japan, Poland, four from Soviet Russia, and two from the United States of America, of whom one was J.Robert Oppenheimer. Kapitsa, however, was Rutherford's protégé. His father had been a general in the corps of engineers; his grandfather had also been a Tsarist general. Penniless after the Bolshevik Revolution and branded a class enemy, he had graduated from Leningrad Polytechnic in electrical engineering and desperately sought a career. His first wife and two children died in an influenza epidemic, but he married Aleksey Krylov's daughter Anna and had two more children. His brilliance was noted by Joffé, his political reliability trusted by the Soviet government. His character made him attractive both to Rutherford and to his colleagues at the Cavendish. C.P.Snow, himself a Cambridge scientist, has left a flattering portrait of Kapitsa in *Variety of Men*:

There was coming and going among laboratories all over the world, including Russia. Peter Kapitsa, Rutherford's favourite pupil, contrived to be in good grace with the Soviet authorities and at the same time a star of the Cavendish. He had a touch of genius: also in those days, before life sobered him, he had a touch of the inspired Russian clown. He loved his own country, but he distinctly enjoyed backing both horses, working in Cambridge and taking his holidays in the Caucasus. He once asked a friend of mine if a foreigner could become an English peer; we strongly suspected that his ideal career would see him established simultaneously in the Soviet Academy of Sciences and as Rutherford's successor in the House of Lords.

Kapitsa's subject of study was the magnetic properties of matter in very strong fields, particularly at low temperatures. He designed and had installed a liquid hydrogen plant, subsidized by funds from the Department of Scientific and Industrial Research. He was aided by another of Rutherford's pupils, John Cockcroft, a textile mill-owner's son, who was to become the director of Britain's atomic research programme, both in Montreal and at Harwell. Through the Royal Society with Rutherford as its President, Kapitsa was made a professor and funds were allocated to build a new Mond laboratory to house a helium liquefier for Kapitsa's low-temperature research, an installation to rival those in Leyden and Strasbourg.

Yet Kapitsa's real contribution to physics came from his club, which met informally on Tuesdays in Trinity College where he held a fellowship. According to J.G.Crowther, a Marxist colleague and a historian of science, the Kapitsa Club with its free-and-easy criticism contributed greatly to the 'valuable thick-skinned Cavendish style'. Kapitsa himself believed in fun in research and in enjoying life. He conducted 'fool-experiments' which sometimes led to important discoveries. He was used to the Russian student tradition of discussing things rather than accepting the wisdom of elders and professors. At the Kapitsa Club many major discoveries were first announced: James Chadwick's finding of the neutron and Cockcroft's research on accelerating charged particles that was, with the help of the Russian George Gamov's theories, first to disintegrate the lithium atom and transmute it to helium.

In terms of fundamental discoveries that would change our understanding of the structure of the world, the interchanges at the

Kapitsa Club made the *conversazione* of the Society of Apostles seem small beer. Science and the technology derived from it would transform human societies, while the military application of atomic research would disturb international relations. Any political or social changes brought about by members of the Apostles could only be trivial. Yet the Apostles had the gift of the pen and the power of the word. They backed into publicity. Their clandestine doings were to become famous. Along with their associates in Bloomsbury, rarely in the field of human endeavour has so much been written about so few who achieved so little. As for the Kapitsa Club, rarely in the field of human discovery has so little been written about so few who achieved so much. It was an admirable illustration of C.P.Snow's famous theory about Two Cultures, in which the more important scientific 'culture' was the less known and appreciated.

There was a fundamental difference between the club and the society. The club of thirty scientists was open to talent. Though discussions there were in confidence, and that confidence was never broken in public, the object was to spread the good news of scientific discovery among those who would apply it to their own research. Kapitsa himself may have had other motives. As Crowther writes in his absorbing history of the Cavendish, despite Rutherford's warning against engaging in Communist propaganda in his laboratory, Kapitsa and his pupils were laying the foundations for a scientific-technical revolution. On his annual visits to Russia after 1929, Kapitsa was retained by the Soviet authorities as an adviser on setting up a Physics Institute in Kharkov. He was to aid in the development of atomic research in the Soviet Union, applied by the state to military and civil purposes. The political revolution sought by some members of the secret Society of Apostles could have little application outside military intelligence, but their aid in direct espionage on nuclear weapons helped to destroy the possibility of the open exchange of scientific knowledge, the aim of the Kapitsa Club.

At the Cavendish Laboratory was another brilliant and striking physicist from a military background, Patrick Blackett, a young naval officer who had served with distinction at the battles of the

Falkland Islands and Jutland. Blackett suffered a radical conversion at Magdalene College, Cambridge, and became an extreme Socialist. With Kapitsa, Blackett formed the core of a group dedicated to discoveries in theoretical physics; his own field of study was nuclear disintegration through use of the Wilson cloud chamber, which led to the discovery of the neutron. Along with Kapitsa, Blackett and Bernal had a strong influence on undergraduates and researchers. They related the funding and the chosen fields of scientific inquiry to the application and social function of science. Pure research was a luxury that poor humanity could not afford. The discovery of new theories should have a good use by a truly Socialist government.

Such thinking was anathema to the representatives of the other tendency of the Apostles and the Bloomsberries. They had discarded utilitarian and social ethics for the creative development of the self. A younger group of influential writers and critics fell under the influence of Bloomsbury, Raymond Mortimer and David Garnett, Harold Nicolson and his wife Vita Sackville-West, Roger Senhouse and Gerald Brenan, and younger dons and Apostles such as the theatrical George ('Dadie') Rylands, who actually played the part of Electra in a Cambridge production of the *Oresteia* and became the guiding spirit of the dramatic group founded by Rupert Brooke, the Marlowe Society. Bloomsbury seemed unforgivably successful, particularly in possessing its own means of production, the Hogarth Press, which published Katherine Mansfield's stories and T.S. Eliot's unsettling *The Waste Land*. It was gradually fixing the standards and tastes of the metropolis and of an élite at the major universities. Worse still, as Quentin Bell pointed out, success seemed to come by divine right from an aristocracy of intellectuals like the privileged Hilberries in Virginia Woolf's novel, *Night and Day*. Although not a secret society, the Bloomsberries were exclusive and fashionable with the private language and the separate behaviour of those who believe themselves born to be arbiters of taste. They gave, in Anthony Powell's opinion, the true twenties' parties: 'The incongruity, touch of homosexuality, intellectuals' astonishment at forms of life other than their own, in combination convey the right period touch.'

Robert Graves had seen two distinct Britains before the Great War and after it. By the end of the twenties, the Britains of the governing and the governed were still there, but the ruling classes were split between those who sought to uphold the old established values and the subversive élites, the Apostles and the Bloomsberries and the group of Oxford wits such as Maurice Bowra, Cyril Connolly and Evelyn Waugh, who used satire to change the ways of their countrymen. In fact, the alternative cultures suggested by the Marxists and by the discoverers of a new science would change the ways of humanity more completely than articulate and exclusive groups that put themselves and the arts above all.

3 Climacteric

At the time of the General Strike in 1926, Maynard Keynes was reflecting on whether he should join the Labour Party. He decided against it. The party was a class party, and the class was not his class. If he was going to pursue sectional interests, he would pursue his own – as a good Apostle or Bloomsberry should. Although he could be influenced by the justice and good sense of the Socialist side, 'the *Class* war will find me on the side of the educated bourgeoisie'.

It was a cogent and clear statement by Keynes, that made sense in the 1920s. The élite at Cambridge was middle class; its prized liberties resulted from a capitalist society which it helped to influence and govern. The poet John Lehmann might notice as an undergraduate at Trinity that the shadow of the Great War still haunted Cambridge, always in the background, conditioning the sensibility; but the storm clouds of another world war had not yet begun to darken the future. It was the seeming failure of capitalism during the great depression and the rise of Fascist governments in Europe that were to make a class war and a world war thinkable to some of the sons of privilege, ashamed of a birthright that began to seem an inherited wrong.

Soviet Russia was still not officially recognized by the British government, which was following Lloyd George's policy of stopping the flow of Bolshevik lava into Europe, but leaving the volcano in Russia to burn itself out. There was a trade treaty between the two countries, but a raid by the Special Branch on the Russian trading company Arcos in 1927 revealed that the mission was used for subversion and propaganda in the interests of the Soviet state.

That was hardly a surprise, although there was no evidence that Russia was purloining British military secrets or had master-minded the General Strike. As a result of the raid, there was an Anglo–Soviet rupture for two years before Ramsay MacDonald restored full diplomatic relations in 1929, when he became Prime Minister for the second time. Within a few years, Britain was Russia's largest market, taking one-third of her annual exports, and helping the Soviets in their ambitious plans for industrialization.

The collapse of the British economy, the rise of unemployment to two and a half million workers by 1931, the international financial crisis and the formation of a National Government appeared to confirm the myth of rule by old men and inadequate men with retrograde values inappropriate for the hard times. Ramsay MacDonald seemed to have betrayed Socialist principles by agreeing to remain as Prime Minister in a coalition government increasingly dominated by Conservatives. The sole possibility of changing the regime appeared to be the undemocratic way of subversion or revolution. The only country standing against the rising totalitarian powers of Italy and Germany and Japan, all loosely called 'Fascist', seemed to be Soviet Russia, also totalitarian under Stalin's leadership, but claiming a dictatorship of the proletariat. The dragon's teeth had been sown in and after the Great War; the myth of the old men who had sacrificed the best young men in the killing grounds of no man's land and had lost the opportunities of peace; the attack on customary values by Bloomsbury that culminated in the rash of anti-war works of the twenties from *What Price Glory?* to *All Quiet on the Western Front*. Commitment to country and to government was devalued; incitement to rebellious self-expression was to become incitement to revolutionary change among part of the Cambridge élite.

In *The Thirties*, Julian Symons correctly defined the middle-class cult of the left as a pyramid with an apex of writers, radical scientists, journalists and documentary film makers. About fifty thousand influential sympathizers and fellow-travellers supported the views of those at the apex and passed them on to an audience of a million people spread out across the country and responsive to the new radical fashions. The masses were hardly touched. The situation

33

was different at Cambridge, where new Communist cells spreading out from Trinity influenced more than a thousand undergraduates to join the Socialist Club by the end of the decade, one in five of the students. Of this thousand, one in four was a member of the Communist Party of Great Britain, which itself grew in the four years after 1933 from eight to twenty thousand members. Julian Bell, the son of Clive and Vanessa Bell, anticipated the future when he wrote to the *New Statesman* in 1933 as a Trinity undergraduate, 'Communism in England is at present very largely a literary phenomenon, an attempt of a second "post-war generation" to escape from the Waste Land.' Contemporary politics were the sole subject of discussion at Cambridge, and 'a very large majority of the more intelligent undergraduates are Communists or almost Communists'. His contemporary at Trinity, John Cornford, repeated the attack in his poem, 'Keep Culture out of Cambridge', with its final lines so far removed from the felicities of Rupert Brooke's 'Granchester':

> There's none of those fashions have come to stay
> And there's nobody here has time to play,
> All we've brought are our party cards
> Which are no bloody good for your bloody charades.

The agents of Marxism at the university were attractive, the conditions for spreading the doctrine suitable. Maurice Dobb had been joined at Trinity by another Communist undergraduate, later a fellow of the college, Anthony Blunt, who was brilliant at philosophy and mathematics, although he chose to specialize in art history. The son of an Anglican clergyman, Blunt had been educated at the public school of Marlborough. After his arrival at Cambridge, he edited an avant-garde literary magazine with Michael Redgrave, *The Venture*. He published the poetry of John Lehmann, Louis MacNeice and Julian Bell, before being elected as an Apostle. He was a homosexual, and was attracted by the *louche* and mercurial Old Etonian Guy Burgess, when he came up to Trinity; Blunt 'fathered' Burgess as an Apostle in 1932, to be joined later by the brilliant Marxist historian Eric Hobsbawm. The society was more and more losing its emphasis on the pursuit of truth and beauty before the onslaught of dialectical materialism. Julian Bell, himself a Trinity

Marxist and an Apostle, regretted the loss of the civilized tongues of his Bloomsbury background from the secret society of King's. Now there was more about the Comintern than *conversazione*, so much so that Maynard Keynes had the regular meetings of the society abrogated, although its Marxist element continued to meet on Saturday evenings. Among their number were many potential recruits to Soviet intelligence, the wealthy young American Michael Whitney Straight, Leo Long, and a rare scientist among the philosophers, Alister Watson.

The driving force behind the spread of Communism at Cambridge among the undergraduates came, however, from the new cell at Trinity College. David Haden-Guest was in revolt from the politics of his father, later ennobled as a Labour peer. He read philosophy under Wittgenstein, but left for a year to go to the University of Göttingen, where he was put in jail for joining a Communist demonstration against the Nazis. He and John Cornford, the son of a renowned Cambridge classical historian, were the active agents in the Trinity cell, which was also joined by the future historian of the British Communist Party, James Klugman. Another member of the cell was the stuttering Kim Philby, the son of a famous Arabist. Two other Communist undergraduates from the neighbouring college of Trinity Hall were occasional visitors; Donald Maclean, also in revolt from his father, a Liberal minister in Ramsay MacDonald's apostate National Government; and the quiet physicist Alan Nunn May, who seemed more committed to his laboratory than to the cause.

Idealism, which drew most of these undergraduates to Marxism, then turned into an ideology. Initially, a tinker's cart of progressive causes attracted bourgeois youths in revolt from the rusty iron hand of their fathers. Sympathy for the poor and the unemployed, pacifism except in the struggle of the United Front against Fascism, a belief in internationalism and the brotherhood of man, a hatred of capitalist arrogance and inefficiency, these mixed feelings led to an attachment to Communism. Michael Whitney Straight in his confessional autobiography, *After Long Silence*, told of living with his brother in a London mansion, looked after by footmen while he attended the London School of Economics, where he had been

35

placed by the Socialist economist Harold Laski. The president of
the student union, an American Communist, persuaded him to
donate twenty pounds to help refugees from Nazi Germany. He
was uprooted with no sense of loyalty to the United States of America
or to Britain. 'I felt alone and isolated ... I was waiting to be re-
claimed. I believed in equality; I feared violence and war.' Straight
was finally recruited for the Communist cause at Trinity,
Cambridge. There the birdlike Klugman and the dark, taut Cornford
worked on Straight's sense of guilt for inheriting a fortune as well
as on his idealism. He joined the university Socialist Club, which
was dominated by Klugman and Cornford, and also the Trinity
Communist cell. He considered himself only a student member of
a student movement. He had no sense of loyalty to the British
Communist Party, which actively directed the actions of Klugman
and Cornford through its leader Harry Pollitt and its national organizer, Douglas Springhall, while the Palme Dutt brothers supervised
the recruitment of the intellectuals.

Straight was conscious of the presence of 'moles' among the student Communists. They were going into the law or the civil service.
They had to appear not to be Marxists in order to be accepted
into their chosen professions. Their deception was considered discretion. Their loyalty lay to the cause of mankind, not to the nation.
There were also 'moles' among the dons, who could not declare
themselves Communists too openly and advance in their calling.
They could influence undergraduates towards Marxism, for, as one
student Socialist leader declared, 'Relations with dons were no
longer based on the false assumption that all Fellows were natural
Fascists.'

One of the 'moles' among the dons was Anthony Blunt, pale
and tall and silent, who accompanied Straight on a tour of Russia
in 1935, yet would disappear on errands of his own. Some of the
student Communists on the Russian tour reacted badly: Charles
Fletcher-Cooke did not like the Soviet system and was to become
a Conservative Member of Parliament. During a visit to the Kremlin, Straight stroked a mantelpiece with reverence, murmuring,
'Soviet timber, Soviet marble,' only to find Fletcher-Cooke shouting
at him, 'Bow down and worship wood and stone! Certainly not.'

Others in the group were not to develop as they should. Michael Young was to join the House of Lords and become a founder of the Social Democratic Party. Only one of the Moscow visitors, Brian Simon, eventually rose to membership of the Central Committee of the British Communist Party.

Another group of foreign students at Cambridge were overt Communists, Party members and organizers. Among them were the witty and charismatic Ceylonese Pieter Keuneman and the old Etonian Indian from King's, S.M.Kumaramangalam, both of whose contributions to the Communist causes in their own countries showed Britain's willingness to educate those who wanted to end its empire. Keuneman was only bested once in a debate when he attacked the British Empire and and was asked by the old Jewish poet and civil servant Humbert Wolfe: 'If you don't like it, why don't you get out?' He never got out, as did the extraordinary Indian from King's, Sri Aurobindo Ghose, who took a First in classics at the university, but ended a mystic and extreme nationalist, suspected of terrorist conspiracy against the Raj between the wars.

The particular event that brought the Communists into the Cambridge streets was the arrival of the Hunger Marchers, unemployed men going to protest at Westminster. Guy Burgess joined their ranks for a few miles on either side of Cambridge, although he would hardly walk all the way from the north of England to London. But it was Straight who prevented them from becoming wayward. As the column took a deviation towards Midsummer Common, the future President of the Cambridge Union Percy Cradock saw Straight heading off the Hunger Marchers in the correct direction, 'leaping along with all the agility with which he had once danced the part of the Dominant Male Principle in the choreography of Sibelius's second symphony.... How could any of us resist this dynamic combination of playboy and Sir Galahad? It took Cornford to bell the cat and say that the real Hunger Marchers were really hungry and did not need rich students playing at guiding them.

The privileged young men at Cambridge, who were attracted to the Communists, still thought of themselves as an élite. But they wanted to become members of a revolutionary élite, not an inherited one. Its ways were clandestine, not by title. They might achieve

37

a secret power, not a public name. They could tunnel and burrow in order to undermine society, not flaunt and fulminate in order to lead it. They were the shock troops of a revolution that imposed a discipline on them and swore them to silence except when the party called on them to demonstrate and make speeches. They were no longer rebels in the cause of self-expression and the assault on custom, without orders, without responsibilities, without fear of consequences, with private means. They were the future leaders of the proletariat. They had left their class to become the vanguard of the masses, with orders, with responsibility, with fear of exposure, without King or Country.

The hidden group and the exclusive club were very much part of their education and their heritage. From the age of eight, boys were separated from their families and herded into preparatory and public schools, which became a substitute for the family. 'The boys sought among their contemporaries affection which they associated with the school,' Noel Annan wrote of Stowe, 'and reciprocated by giving their hearts to the place.' From the self-electing 'Pop' of gaudy prefects at Eton who ran the college, through the innumerable societies at Oxford and Cambridge, of which the Apostles and the Communist cells were secret ones, through to the London clubs and the Masonic lodges so powerful in the world of business, an Englishman from the privileged classes expected to achieve a male bonding exclusive of others, even of his own peers, certainly of the other sex.

Exclusion was a principle in the creation of the English governing cliques. As Bertrand Russell said of the Apostles, secrecy was necessary 'in order that those being considered for election may be unaware of the fact'. Moreover, Apostles had to protect themselves from those who wanted to join them. Yet sometimes more important than those who were brought in were those who were kept out. The blackball was the cement of the club. Clandestine association was an intellectual aphrodisiac, inducing closet ways and a sense of innate superiority. To be an Apostle was not only to be among the best, but to be set apart in splendid stealthiness, like the invisible worm that flew in the night in the poem by William Blake – an artist praised by Anthony Blunt for his escape from the dominance of materialism and his complete integrity of thought and feeling – qualities which Blunt himself only appeared to share.

The Apostles were a latter-day Platonic society. They saw themselves as the undeclared guardians of English culture. They never questioned their right and their duty to influence the worlds of art and politics, or to prefer other Apostles into posts of influence, particularly in the academic field. Their Plato's Cave was a room in King's and, like Plato's philosopher, they could distinguish between the fire and the shadow on the wall, the meaning of truth and materialism, the real and the phenomenal. When invaded by Communists who declared that the real world was the material one, they were not too dismayed. It was an aberration of the thirties, a temporary dialectic rather than a formal logic. Just as Marx had stood Hegel on his head, so the Marxists were standing Plato on his tools. Both the followers of G.E.Moore and of Communism, however, usually shared important characteristics: a love of secrecy and its powers, a desire to aid one another, a passionate puritanism from the English tradition, an abhorrence of the greater world, an inversion into their own society, an arrogance about their quality and, above all, the double language of the Jesuits, the words spoken to other Apostles seeking the truth, and the words spoken to the masses outside, who could not understand the truth.

All Apostles, when accepted into the society, had to swear a fearful oath that their soul would writhe in unendurable pain for all eternity if they were to betray the society to anyone not a member. Similar oaths were sworn by Masons and the secret revolutionary societies such as the Jacobins, at whose time of trial the Conversazione Society was founded. When Michael Straight swore the oath in Keynes's rooms, it seemed a bit harsh, but the Provost of King's assured him that it had been written at a time when it was unlikely that an Apostle would speak to anyone who was not one. It was that exclusive and self-regarding a society. As to what an Apostle was, Straight was assured by the Provost of King's, John Tressider Sheppard, 'One must be *very* brilliant and *extremely* nice!'

One also had to be very clandestine and extremely selective. In a phrase that became notorious, the Apostle E.M.Forster declared that if he had to choose between betraying his country and betraying

his friend, he hoped he should have the guts to betray his country.
It was not an unqualified statement; it was prefaced by the remark
that he hated the idea of causes. He had truly reacted from the
slaughterhouse patriotism of the First World War into a belief in
personal loyalty and love. He was also a homosexual, and a homosexual friend in their private and illegal communion was certainly
more in need of loyalty than a conventional country. When Forster
described his Apostolic and covert homosexual friend Lowes Dickinson as a tortured humanitarian, he was describing himself. He was
no Marxist: he supported free speech and democracy, he did not
confuse loving working men individually with loving the masses.

The strong homosexual element among the Apostles did buttress
their oath of secrecy and separate them more from conventional
society. To be an open homosexual was to ruin one's career and
risk legal prosecution and prison. To stay in the closet was necessary
in the outer world, but unnecessary in the inner world of truth
among the Apostles. It encouraged a double vision and a double
language. Those Marxists who were homosexuals were even more
tightly bound together in worlds of subterfuge and deceit. They
could betray neither their party nor their friends to their disapprov-
ing countrymen. With a blindness that defies belief, they chose
not to know the fact that Stalinist Russia persecuted homosexuals
even more than England did. It may have led an André Gide to
denounce it, but an Anthony Blunt preferred to ignore it.

Homosexuality, indeed, reinforced the closeness of the Communist conspiracy. It was a tool of recruitment as well as a mechanism
of control, a second threat of exposure to an alien and capitalist
environment. Anthony Blunt certainly shared his sexual preferences
as well as his ideology with Guy Burgess. When Michael Straight
met them both together in Trinity he recorded a sense of 'the terrible
significance of it all'. He felt violent, uncontrollable love for his
Communist friends, such as Cornford and Klugman and Maurice
Dobb, although it was not physical. 'It burns within me and I
can't express it; I can't get it out.'

A double-talk, a double-think, a double life created the conditions
for becoming an agent with dual loyalties. Cornford and Klugman
regularly met Harry Pollitt, the leader of the Communist Party

of Great Britain and his national organizer, Douglas Springhall, who reported to Samuel Borisovich Cahan, the chief recruiting agent for Soviet spies in England. Cornford and Klugman were members of the Trinity cell, where Blunt probably recruited Burgess as a Soviet agent, although he later declared to British intelligence that the younger Burgess recruited him. Blunt certainly tried to turn Michael Straight into a Russian agent. He instructed Straight that the Communist International ordered the rich American to stage a nervous breakdown, leave the Party, go underground and become a mole in Wall Street. Straight accepted the assignment; he moved from the crowded noisy world of Cambridge into a world of shadows and echoes; he was 'on the other side of the mirror by then'. Burgess also recruited the bisexual Donald Maclean, claiming to have seduced him as well. Maclean was then an open Communist sympathizer, spending most of his time on Party activities, and writing attacks in the undergraduate magazine *Granta* on the capitalist, dictatorial character of the university. Only later was he instructed to become a mole and join the diplomatic service.

Homosexuality did not turn a Cambridge intellectual towards the clandestinity and hidden power game of Communism, but it helped. Entry into a Marxist conspiracy, in a contemporary Apostolic phrase, was rather through the Homintern than the Comintern, even though most Apostles preferred Sodom to Moscow and Gomorrah to Leningrad. Ludwig Wittgenstein, for instance, was a homosexual and no Christian, yet his philosophic scruples kept him, like Maynard Keynes, a long way from the influence of Leninism despite his admiration of Russia. In his article on Anthony Blunt, 'The Cleric of Treason', George Steiner has suggested that Judaism and homosexuality, most intensely where they overlapped in the case of a Wittgenstein or a Proust, could be seen to have been two main generators in the fabric of modern urbanity. They increased the sense of separation from nation and from common values. This was not so in C. P. Snow's other 'culture' of scientists and mathematicians. Only the genius Alan Turning, who restructured Algebra and Number Theory while a young fellow of King's, and later became a leading code-breaker at Bletchley during the Second World War, was to die of cyanide poisoning after being convicted in Manchester as a practising homosexual. As his biographer states, Turing found himself to be an ordinary English homosexual atheist mathematician. What was acceptable in King's at Cambridge, outside might prove illegal, if not fatal.

Keynes's biographer Skidelsky and the playwright and don Alan Bennett have both stressed the quintessential Englishness of the Apostles and of the few traitors among them. Their exclusiveness and secrecy were inherited from the practices of an élite. The selection process which made them Apostles was elaborate and began with their birth. Bennett called the Cambridge traitors of the thirties 'English to excess'. They were proud of their inheritance of irony and scepticism. 'To be dubious about that inheritance was to be part of that inheritance.' To mock one's country was to prove one's right to mock it. Bennett quoted W.H.Auden saying that if he had been more clever, he would have been a criminal or a spy. In fact, Auden's going to America for the duration of the Second World War was considered a treachery, a desertion of duty.

Intellectual snobbery and a sense of drama were other attractions to the coterie at King's in the thirties. That Cambridge college was not only the home of the Apostles, but also the social and intellectual centre of the university. Its fellows led in the fields of economics and philosophy, classics and literature, although they did not join especially in the new criticism being developed by I.A.Richards, a kind of Apostolic scrutiny of the meaning of poems and the reasons for enjoying them. Richards had, however, studied under Wittgenstein, who always reminded him of Lucifer, because he looked like the Devil and was a dab hand at sowing discord.

It was in the theatre that Donald Beves and George Rylands, aided by Maynard Keynes in his founding of the Arts Theatre in honour of his ballerina wife, Lydia Lopokova, made King's the arbiter of university drama. The epicene Beves was to be falsely named as the Fourth Man among the Cambridge Soviet spies; but as he used to say when a disaster struck one of his Cambridge productions, 'These little things are sent to try us.' Rylands directed Michael Redgrave in 1932 in *Captain Brassbound's Conversion*: the décor was by Guy Burgess, who early developed the sense of drama which Auden wished on a young relation.

So I wish you first a
Sense of theatre: only
Those who love illusion
      And know it will go far:
Otherwise we spend our
Lives in a confusion
Of what we say and do with
      Who we really are.

Guy Burgess loved the illusion of Soviet Russia and went as far as it told him to go. Arguably, he was to spend his life in a confusion of what he said and did with who he really was. So did many of his contemporaries, who also had a young man's sense of drama and were born in the Marxist climate of parts of Cambridge in the thirties. Theatrical success had long been a criterion of success itself at the university. It encouraged a love of disguise, of playing many parts other than one's own true self. It enhanced a feeling of cleverness, increased if asked by a George Rylands or an Anthony Blunt to join a secret society, which certainly thought its members to be cleverer than other people and better as well. 'Is it monomania?' Maynard Keynes once demanded of Lytton Strachey – the colossal sense of moral superiority that the Apostles felt. 'Most of the rest never see anything at all – too stupid or too wicked.'

The Communists of the thirties, indeed, felt even more moral superiority than the non-Communists. There was no question that they were the heirs of the puritans and the evangelicals, who wanted a new heaven on a new earth. They supported the only society which knew how to produce it materially, Soviet Russia, while all other societies were crashing to economic ruin. It was only two decades later that Bertrand Russell, in his essay, 'Why I Am Not a Communist', could state that he was at a loss to understand how some people who were both humane and intelligent could find something to admire in the vast slave camp produced by Stalin. But at the time, it appeared to the left to be a laboratory forging a fresh human society; so much so that the young Marxist Cambridge student Charles Madge could parody William Wordsworth with the jejune intensity of these lines printed in *New Country*:

43

> Lenin, would you were living at this hour:
> England has need of you, of the cold voice
> That spoke beyond Time's passions, that expelled
> All the half treasons of the mind in doubt.

Wordsworth's selfish men were the old men in government and the older Apostles, who still believed, like E.M.Forster, in the pursuit of personal truth. Their half treasons were to question the brave new world being set up by the Soviet system and the commitment to discipline demanded by a belief in Marxism. They should not submit Stalin's Russia to Apostolic scrutiny: they should approve it, warts, treason trials and all. The road to the future was the road to Moscow. It demanded belief without a mind in doubt. Even the distinction between British Socialism and Soviet Communism became blurred among some of the best minds. Leading Socialists like John Strachey could declare to the Cambridge Union that a Communist was a Socialist who meant what he said; there was no split between the two movements in doctrine. Such a fudge of the political truth might result in Popular Front movements against Fascism leading later to vicious strife between temporary alliances of incompatible left-wing groups; but it was a heady drug for young minds in search of a united commitment by all radicals against the aggressions of Hitler, the injustice of mass unemployment, and the invulnerability of the incompetent and guilty men, as Michael Foot termed them, who seemed to govern Britain by reducing it to a state of paralysis. Religion might once have been the opium of the people, but now Marxism was the opium of the bourgeois idealists, who sought to end war, poverty, inequality and privilege.

The militant writers and philosophers of the left saw Stalin's Russia of Gulag and forced collectivization as a pipe-dream of factory and electricity and peace. They thought he was changing the world; they did not choose to see how nor did they know how. Those material details they left to the scientists, of whom they knew little or nothing. And some of those leading scientists were committed enough to see the same eastern visions as hard facts, not just as fond words. As Professor Lancelot Hogben asserted in his popular *Science and the Citizen*, 'This is not the age of pamphleteers. It is

44

the age of engineers. The spark-gap is mightier than the pen. Democracy will not be salvaged by men who talk fluently, debate forcefully and quote aptly.' Scientists would change society. Nobody else.

They were already making a powder of the universe. In the twenties, Maxwell's explanations of electromagnetism and Einstein's of gravity suggested new fundamental laws for matter and energy. There appeared to be only two atomic particles, the proton with its electrons swinging round it. Einstein expected soon to discover a unified theory. Physics would be over in six months, Max Born declared. Then James Chadwick found the neutron, to be followed by the discovery of the positron and dozens of other atomic particles without apparent direction or significance. These were to be called quarks from James Joyce's *Finnegan's Wake* because of their random and anarchic nature. Physics no longer seemed to explain the world, but to disintegrate it. The basics of all matter seemed arbitrary and contradictory, just as most human societies did.

4 An Excess of Generosity

The Apostles in their long history excluded all the notable Cambridge scientists, Darwin and Jeans, Eddington and Galton. They were little interested in that alternative culture, however important it was in changing the world and other people's perceptions of the world. Their view was shared by most of the leading figures in the arts at Cambridge. As the illustrious mathematician G. H. Hardy said to C. P. Snow, the word 'intellectual' as used by literary intellectuals in the thirties seemed to have a new definition. It did not include Rutherford or Eddington or Dirac or Adrian or himself. 'It does seem rather odd, don't y' know.'

Hardy himself happened to be one of the rare mathematicians interested in science who was an Apostle. There were a few others, notably Alister Watson, twice secretary to the society, who was as much an admirer of Lenin as Hardy was. Two other secretaries to the society were scientists from King's, the American William Grey Walter, who became a leader in studies in electroencephalography and clinical neurophysiology and cybernetics, and David Champernowne, a mathematician and statistician who worked with Alan Turing on the basics of computer science. They were supported by another Apostle, the moral philosopher Richard Braithwaite, who was also interested in the philosophy of science. Two other biophysicists were influential members of the society in the late thirties: Victor (later Lord) Rothschild, and Alan Hodgkin, later knighted and elected Master of Trinity. But these few mathematicians and scientists were rare bridges across the divide between the 'two cultures' at Cambridge.

In a collection of essays on the state of the arts and sciences, called *Cambridge University Studies* and published in 1933, for once the scientists had the better of the battle of words. Both Patrick Blackett and C.P.Snow wrote articles for the volume. Blackett did not mention his political convictions. He wrote of the methods of scientific discovery, calling an experimental physicist a jack-of-all-trades. He must not only be a thinker and a mathematician with a knowledge of quantum mechanics, but also a versatile craftsman, who must blow glass, be a carpenter, turn metal, photograph, wire electrical circuits, and master gadgets of all kinds. Everything had to be done on a shoe-string. Red Bank of England sealing wax was regularly used as vacuum cement; plasticine sealed the great tubes needed to disintegrate elements by fast protons. He emphasized the practical side of theoretical discovery. Man, as in Marxist biology, was primarily a tool-using animal, a worker with hands and brain. Blackett underlined the Cavendish's concern in investigating the structure and disintegration of heavy radioactive nuclei. He did not mention that such a release of energy would be the prerequisite for the construction of an atomic weapon.

C.P.Snow's article dealt with chemistry, but was more illuminating. The proper study of chemistry was the structure of molecules and of their reactions in combinations with one another. Snow stressed that the future of chemistry at Cambridge rested with physics and that it was following the same tendency as in the rest of the world: 'To do otherwise would be original; it would also be ridiculous.' There should be no essential difference between chemistry in Cambridge, Oxford, London, Berlin or Pasadena – or indeed, by implication, in Moscow. Science was unique among professions. Each scientist knew every other scientist working in his own field by name and research done – and often personally. Only Rutherford and Niels Bohr had anticipated the normal progress of their time by twenty years. Bohr himself was almost a surrogate son of Rutherford, a Dane with the bulging forehead of the traditional intellectual, the director of the Institute for Theoretical Physics at Copenhagen. Coming from a small, disengaged country, he evoked no national prejudices, and British and French, Russian and American physicists passed through Copenhagen as through a neutral zone. Bohr was the first to aid the German-Jewish scientists who were fleeing Nazi Germany; he was supported by Rutherford's Academic Assistance Council and by the Royal Society in finding them places in England. One of Hitler's greater mistakes was to force that exodus of refugees. One in four of Germany's leading physicists and fifteen hundred of her leading scholars lost their posts and went into exile in Hitler's first two years of power. Before that terrible exclusion, it had been the golden age of science, when the Cambridge physicists had believed that all knowledge should be shared by the researchers from all the nations of the earth. The very word science derived from *scientia*, meaning knowledge. Modern science was organized knowledge and a method of empirical validation that knew no national boundaries. The proper use of science lay in the proper exchange of that knowledge. Science was a collective pursuit. 'We need all the cosmopolitanism that we can get,' C.P.Snow declared. 'There is no danger of an excess of generosity.'

Remarkably, the outspoken Socialist Blackett did not write of sharing knowledge in theoretical physics and nuclear fission, even though he was soon to declare that scientists must be directly concerned with the great political struggle of the day, that the only way of the future was complete Socialism. It was C.P.Snow who championed the sharing of theoretical knowledge in physics and chemistry, even if it might have an industrial or military use. Two traditions in intellectual research were represented. Firstly, the committed position, which believed in providing information for ideological reasons. There could be no treason in transmitting scientific discoveries to people of like mind engaged in building theoretically a better and more equal society, because such information transcended frontiers and nationalism. The second tradition dated from the foundation of Cambridge University and all universities, that advances in knowledge should be shared with all mankind. The integrity of the scholar demanded the disclosure of his discoveries to help all in the common pursuit of wisdom. A little learning might be a dangerous thing: a shared learning was an essential thing. The danger for researchers and nations lay in mutual suspicion and in secrecy in the name of security. There was no danger in an excess of generosity.

Such admirable beliefs could be misconstrued in an interval between global wars and in an age of intelligence gathering and extreme political conviction and antagonism. The Bolsheviks had declared a world revolution. As with the early Christians, a man was with it or against it. To be a fellow-traveller was not always enough, particularly when the rise of Adolf Hitler in 1933 produced a Fascist power in Germany potentially stronger than Mussolini's Italy and apparently dedicated to the overthrow of Bolshevism.

With the great depression in capitalist countries, the apparent success of the Soviet Five-Year Plans with full employment, and the rise of aggressive Fascist powers, there was a change in the thinking of radical scientists in the early 1930s. A climacteric was the Second International Congress of the History of Science and Technology, held in London in July 1931. A Russian scientific delegation appeared, led by Nikolay Ivanovich Bukharin, the foremost Bolshevik theorist after Lenin; his expulsion two years before from the Politburo and the chairmanship in the Communist International was still unknown. With him were the physicist Joffé and the eminent plant geneticist N.I.Vavilov. Secretly, Bukharin was charged by Stalin to persuade Kapitsa to return permanently to his homeland, but Kapitsa would not commit himself. Openly at the conference Bukharin emphasized the union of science with technology and with the organization of production. The whole world was already divided into two economic systems, two forms of social relationships, two types of culture. The economic decline of capitalism was reflected in crises of scientific thought and philosophy. The new intellectual and scientific culture of Soviet Russia was the pattern of the future.

This radical and hopeful message appealed to many of the scientists, particularly to the Communists Desmond Bernal, J.G.Crowther and Hyman Levy, and to the Soviet sympathizers, Blackett, Joseph Needham, Jack Haldane, Julian Huxley and Lancelot Hogben. These eminent young British scientists were to be a great influence on contemporary students; all became members that year of the Tots and Quots dining club; none of them was to protest when the Soviet Union detained Kapitsa to work in Russia. 'There is no one in politics today', the Apostle John Maynard

Keynes wrote, 'worth sixpence outside the ranks of the liberals except the post-war generation of intellectual Communists under thirty-five. Them, too, I like and respect.' In their feelings and instincts, they reminded Keynes of the nonconformists who went on the Crusades, made the Reformation, fought the English Civil War, and won civil and religious liberties for their countrymen.

As an early Communist at Cambridge with only the little group led by Maurice Dobb as secret sharers, Desmond Bernal had found himself somewhat isolated. He was a big man of captivating charm, in the opinion of the Peterhouse historian Herbert Butterfield, and certainly influenced hundreds of undergraduates. Some of that influence was through the organization of an anti-war group within the local branch of the Association for Scientific Workers. This group protested against the use of scientific research for rearmament, and attracted the support of many liberals including C. P. Snow: pacifists of the time were not necessarily Marxists.

Other leading Soviet sympathizers at Cambridge were the biologist Jack Haldane and the biochemist Joseph Needham, who declared that Communist leaders emerged from within – this dealt with the problem of the dictatorship of Joseph Stalin, who was already holding show trials of scientists and would eliminate in due course both Bukharin and N. I. Vavilov, accused of being a British agent. Needham considered that only Fascist leaders were imposed from above. His curious Christian Marxism denied the persecution of religion and state control of science in Russia. He did not see what he did not wish to see, believing that Communism, in a sense, completed and extended Christianity. It was also a biological imperative, for advanced life was essentially organization and order.

His confusion of thought was not shared by most of the leading radical scientists, who went on a tour of Russia organized by Crowther in 1931. Haldane and Huxley were part of the group, as was Cockcroft. Bernal, Haldane and Huxley were entranced by Russian planning and industrialization and dialectical materialism. As Huxley wrote in his book, *A Scientist Among the Soviets*:

Other nations may not follow the same paths as Russia. They may be able to reorganize their disordered systems without having recourse either to open revolution or to orthodox communism. But whatever new course they pursue (and it is abundantly clear that they cannot continue on the old course) they cannot help learning much from Russia. The technique and the very idea of large-scale planning: the socialization of agriculture: the reduction of private profit and class distinction: the provision of peacetime incentives which shall on the one hand not be merely individualist, and on the other not be centred mainly on the crude worship of national power: the elevation of science and scientific method to its proper place in affairs – in these and many other ways the new Russia, even in its present embryo stage of development, is in advance of other countries: and if the rest of the world refuses to learn from the object-lesson provided by Russia, as well as profiting by her mistakes, so much the worse for the rest of the world.

Huxley was not, however, as extreme as Bernal, who supported the state control of scientific research so that the researchers could be directed to work only on what directly benefited the masses.

Bernal had already made major discoveries in X-ray crystallography and the structure of molecules. Without this work, the genetic breakthroughs of the nineteen-fifties would have been stillborn. Even more seminal was Cockcroft and Walton's successful construction of an apparatus to bombard lithium atoms with accelerated protons, causing disintegration. The quiet Cockcroft was seen walking through Cambridge announcing to strangers: 'We've split the atom! We've split the atom!' Lord Rutherford found the splitting of the atom so disturbing that he forbade the publication of the results until they had been proved; only the Kapitsa Club members heard of Cockcroft's research in progress. The implications of this discovery were devastating. Such a release of atomic energy could cause a vast explosion. As Cockcroft's apparatus was handmade and elementary, its development into producing a chain reaction was hypothetical. To dampen press speculation about the consequences of splitting the atom, Rutherford declared in 1933 that the world was not to expect a new source of energy as a practical application of these nuclear experiments. Niels Bohr agreed with him, as did

Einstein. They were being pessimistic or deluding themselves or deluding the press. They did not delude Kapitsa or those of like mind. Cockcroft himself was reasonably optimistic that much more atomic energy could be released by splitting a heavy nucleus. C.P.Snow called Rutherford's wrong judgement about atomic fission the only major scientific bloomer he ever made: 'It is interesting that we should be at the point where pure science turned into applied. No, pure scientists did not show much understanding or display much sense of social fact.'

The civilized world also seemed to be disintegrating along with the atom. The collapse of the free economies of America and Europe along with mass unemployment persuaded many that the future lay with planned economies, either Communist or Fascist. Fascism itself and its aggressive expansion made many radicals shift from pacifism and support of disarmament to anti-Fascism and recognition of the need for rearmament. Significantly, the Politburo decided to recall from abroad its most successful physicist. In 1934, on his annual visit to Russia, Peter Kapitsa was not allowed to return to his new laboratory at Cambridge. When Rutherford heard of this, he warned the Russian ambassador in London that Kapitsa's detention would damage scientific relations between Britain and Russia. The ambassador replied that the success of the First Five-Year Plan and the prosecution of the Second had created a shortage of scientific workers. Soviet scientists abroad were needed at home. 'Mr. Kapitsa belongs to this category. He has now been offered highly responsible work in his particular field in the Soviet Union, which will enable him to develop fully his abilities as a scientist and a citizen of his country.'

There was a parallel between the treatment of scientists by Hitler and by Stalin. Hitler wished for 'Aryan' science to be purged of 'Jewish' science: Stalin believed there was a dialectical opposition between 'proletarian' and 'bourgeois' science. Neither leader of his country had any respect for academic integrity or freedom of movement. Hitler expelled his leading scientists because of their heritage, although Jews had won a quarter of the Nobel Prizes awarded to Germany and held one out of every eight professorial posts. Stalin, however, was determined to recall all Russian émigré scientists to put them to forced labour on the economic development of their homeland. It was necessary for them to prove their loyalty, especially if they were like Kapitsa and came from a family of enemies of the working class.

Arthur Koestler noticed that the obsession of all Communist intellectuals from the middle classes was the cult of the proletarian and the abuse of themselves:

> We were in the Movement on sufferance, not by right; this was rubbed into our consciousness night and day. We had to be tolerated, because Lenin had said so, and because Russia could not do without the doctors, engineers and scientists of the pre-revolutionary intelligentsia, and without the hated foreign specialists.

But Communist bourgeois intellectuals were no more trusted and respected than useful Jews in the Third Reich, saved from the gas-chamber because of special knowledge that could serve the state. The 'Aryans' of the Communist Party were the proletarians, and the social origin of parents and grandparents as workers was as important in applying for membership as Aryan descent was for the Nazi Party.

Peter Kapitsa was doubly damned by his Tsarist government origins and his many years spent abroad. His detention in Russia was finally determined by George Gamov's refusal to return from a scientific congress in Brussels. Kapitsa was considered a hostage for the other leading Russian physicist. According to one witness, the Soviet Minister responsible for the decision said: 'We do not believe that Kapitsa, once he got back to Cambridge, would ever want to come back here, or anyhow if he didn't we couldn't compel him. We badly need our good scientists just now. Why not send us a few good English scientists?' Another witness reported a bitter joke from Kapitsa, who said that he felt like a raped woman who would have given herself for love.

His situation was further damaged by the trial of and sentence of six British engineers working in Russia who were charged with spying and sabotage. It was a trial, as Malcolm Muggeridge reported, at which everything was true except the facts. The engineers had been working for the Metropolitan Vickers Company, which had a large contract to supply turbines and other electrical equipment to the Soviet Union. Unfortunately, Kapitsa had dealt with Metrovick in equipping his low-temperature Mond laboratory and had been subsidized by state funds from the British Department of Scientific and Industrial Research. Rutherford himself had been amazed that Kapitsa had the engineering skills to design a machine for his laboratory which Metrovick could construct from his drawings and which worked. In addition, Kapitsa had even used his research to enter a patent for using intense magnetic fields for increasing the velocity and precision of shells fired from artillery. In the paranoia of Stalinist Russia at the time, Kapitsa appeared to be a Russian who was working on military secrets for a foreign power, secrets which might benefit his own country. His low-temperature research, anyway, had important industrial applications in providing cheap oxygen as well as helium for airships and zeppelins. His experience in electrical engineering was a necessity for a society that believed human progress was a derivative of cheap power.

Rutherford finally broke his diplomatic silence and pointed out that the Soviet government could not force Kapitsa to work well for it. A man could be ordered to become a good bricklayer, but not a great physicist, if he was separated from his laboratory, family and colleagues. Kapitsa was particularly valuable because he was both a theoretical physicist and a mechanic. He could make his concepts. But his apparatus was all in the Mond laboratory at Cambridge. And separated from it and from his family, Kapitsa refused to work in Moscow.

He wrote hundreds of letters to his wife, the daughter of another Russian scientist. Openly, he revealed his loneliness and his thoughts. If compelled to stay in Moscow, he wished to switch to biophysics and work with Pavlov. 'They think that planting me here they can create science,' he complained. 'With a stick one can only make the man dig in the ground and not to do scientific discoveries.' If he had remained a good Socialist and son of his country for thirteen years in England, he would remain so in the future. He wanted to take part in the scientific revolution in Russia, but it was not yet. 'The position of pure science, if not completely nil, is not far from it.' Russia was being rebuilt at a terrific pace, but on a base of imitation of western technology. Interpreters were needed, not original creators. State control and bureaucracy stifled all. 'What in England is done by a telephone call, here requires hundreds of papers. You are trusted in nothing.' Although the Socialist method of economy was the rational model, it was not being achieved rightly. He would obey the commands of the government, because he believed that it was a proletarian government working for the good of the people, but some of the orders sounded 'as if Beethoven was called and told to write the 4th Symphony, by order'.

Yet the passing of the useless months changed Kapitsa's mind. A year after his detention, he wrote to Anna that he must bend his head as a victim of the time. He had been a dead volcano for too long. The 'Arabian Nights scheme' of the transfer of all the equipment from the Mond laboratory to Moscow was now possible. Two old Cambridge colleagues, Professors Adrian and Dirac, visited him in Russia and began the negotiations for removing all his equipment. In a remarkable show of international good feeling and a belief in the pursuit of research at all costs, the Cambridge authorities agreed in 1935 to sell the contents of Kapitsa's laboratory to the Russian government for £30,000. A committee reported to the Council of the Senate, the ruling body at Cambridge, that it was anxious to help Kapitsa to continue in Russia the successful work undertaken in England. Kapitsa knew of the shortages in Russia and insisted that even the clocks and wall fittings were removed from the Mond laboratory; Rutherford remarked that his protégé wanted the paint scraped off the walls. His research assistant Emil Laurmann and his chief mechanic were to accompany the shipment and help to install the equipment over the next three years in Russia. The various pieces of machinery were loaded on to three separate ships taking different routes in case the British government intervened to stop their export. The chief Russian intelligence agent in London, S.B.Cahan, was the organizer of these special methods of shipment and the paymaster of the whole operation. He eventually persuaded Kapitsa's wife that it was safe for her to rejoin her husband in Russia.

'Some of my friends here call me Pickwick,' Kapitsa wrote in a letter of appreciation to Rutherford. 'I take the people better than they are and they think of me worse than I am.' His Institute for Physical Problems was attached to the Soviet Academy of Sciences, which governed his research programmes and funding. His old mentor Abram Joffé, who had ignored him until then, 'suddenly burst out in kindness'. As the leader of physics in general in the Soviet Union, he needed Kapitsa to help in creating a cyclotron to split atoms and proceed to the problem of enriching uranium to produce a bomb.

Kapitsa, as C. P. Snow later testified, was to remain in touch with his fellow scientists in Cambridge, a research relationship and a sharing of knowledge promoted by Snow himself. 'His friendship with Cockcroft and others', Snow wrote, 'meant that the link between Soviet and English science was never quite broken, even in the worst days.' Cockcroft was instrumental and remained important in getting Kapitsa all the equipment that he needed from England. Kapitsa begged him and other Cambridge friends to visit 'the man behind the bars'. He had a deep sense of gratitude in his heart.

These were still the days when the possible military use of atomic research was only surmised by the few, when the excesses of Stalin's purges and forced collectivization were hardly known outside Russia, and when the fight against unemployment and Fascism was the natural cause of brave young minds. To radical scientists with the technological future in their hands the Soviet system was dominant. They had seen the future. It lay in Russia, and it worked. They might not choose to see that the façade of the Russian revolution contradicted its reality; its rhetoric, called dialectic, bore little relation to its effect; its materialism promised a heaven on earth for the proletariat without achieving it. All sacrifices were for the next generation. All failings were the consequence of the hostility of the encircling capitalist and Fascist powers. So a belief was created that it was good to offer scientific knowledge to an opposed ideology and economic system, although dedicated to world revolution. More important to the future of Europe than *La trahison des clercs* or the treachery of the few Cambridge Communists who joined the British diplomatic and intelligence services were the fellow-travellers of the laboratory and the Kapitsa Club.

Because of the willingness of British scientists to share advances in knowledge, it was less necessary for Russian intelligence to engage in espionage of theoretical discoveries. In fact, these had to be closely scrutinized. When Dirac's important *Principles of Quantum Mechanics* was published in Russia in 1932, its introduction warned that many of Dirac's opinions contradicted dialectical materialism and should be used only as material for an attack on idealism. Western theories were dangerous, but easily available; they were useful to assault capitalism. The practical application of these ideas, however, their industrial and military uses, could only be attained through friendly specialists or professional spies. There the frontiers of ethical behaviour, political ideology and academic integrity became confused for many scientists as well as politicians and civil servants. The line between the fellow-traveller, the sympathizer and the occasional agent for a foreign power was a nice line, but unclear.

Three conditions turned the volunteer of information into the spy: payment for intelligence work, the choice of specific appointments with access to secret material, and the procurement of plans and items designated by Russian intelligence. This was to be the role of later Cambridge scientists who were Communists, such as Allan Nunn May. But their contribution in the 1930s was as nothing compared to the open and continuous exchange of theoretical information between Kapitsa and the leading physicists of his age, at Cambridge and Copenhagen and elsewhere.

Too much emphasis is placed on the rare cases of scientists' delivering secret material to foreign agents. The truth is that the interchange of scientific theory and practice was and is common in Europe and America. Nine-tenths of economic and scientific intelligence is performed by the careful scrutiny of academic and technical papers, journals and publications. But such facts are undramatic and diminish intelligence budgets as well as newspaper and book sales. One man's spy is another man's educated reader. One man's double agent is another man's scientist of integrity who believes in universal human progress.

In his disillusioned article on the reasons why he gave up

57

Communism, Stephen Spender commented on the leading Marxist scientists, Jack Haldane and Desmond Bernal. He was convinced that they saw Russia as a country where scientists were highly paid and respected and given vast sums for their research by the state, research which could not be exploited for profit by big businessmen. Haldane himself struck Spender as an eccentric who indulged in heroic self-display and delighted in scientific adventure, while Bernal was inspired with a social passion for the planning of human beings. Yet both appeared slightly inhuman, ready to turn society into a vast field for human experiment without protecting it from the misuse of their discoveries.

> When there is mention of their being responsible for destructive inventions they take refuge in their position as pure scientists. ... Modern science has produced no reason to prevent science from being directed by governments towards purposes of enormous destruction in every country. Science is simply an instrument, for good or for bad. For it to be directed towards good, whoever directs it must have some conception of humanity wider than that of a planned scientific society. There must be a purpose in society beyond good planning. Without such a purpose, to submit society to a dictatorship for the purpose of planned science is simply to lay down the lines for another misuse of science. For in Russia it is the politicians who plan the science.

When Bernal, Haldane and the French physicist Joliot-Curie became and remained members of the Communist Party, Spender was sceptical that they had any other motive than a blind faith in the instrument of science. Yet that instrument had no moral purpose. They seemed ready to put it into the hands of politicians equally ready to persecute scientists who produced results contrary to the political views of the state. To Spender, these Communist scientists were victims of a kind of moral blindness which had long characterized science, but was not to be excused for that reason.

5 The Moles and the Trojan Horse

'In those days', the Communist agent Alexander Foote asserted, 'Spanish affairs divided themselves into right and wrong for me – as, indeed, I think they did for everyone.' The Spanish Civil War, in Robert Graves's opinion, could be seen in many ways: Fascism against Communism, or totalitarianism against democracy; Italy and Germany against England, France and Russia; force against freedom; an army rebellion against a constitutional government; barbarism against culture or Catholicism against atheism; even order against anarchy – 'however one's mind worked'. Few young men's minds worked coherently over the murderous problem, which polarized emotions as well as opinion. Nearly all progressives supported the Republican government, while some conservatives such as Katharine Stewart-Murray, the 'Red Duchess' of Atholl, also backed the legitimate side. The opportunity was heaven-sent to the Communist Party of Great Britain, which became hell-bent on recruiting comrades to serve in the International Brigades in the war. Its Help-for-Spain rallies even made it begin to seem a popular political party. The non-intervention policy of the National Government in England led by Stanley Baldwin was supported by the official Labour Party, although militant Socialists such as Harold Laski called for intervention and a popular front against Fascism. The Communists, indeed, appeared to stand for the democratic ideals of the Spanish Republican government, until George Orwell and Arthur Koestler and other writers in Spain were to disclose how the Party there decimated opposition within its own ranks as well as fighting the enemy outside. To them, a Popular Front was a Communist Front, which used the stab in the back.

The majority of those serving in all the International Brigades in the Spanish Civil War were Communists. In the British battalion, many were miners, few were academics. Cambridge sent some volunteers, Oxford fewer, Bloomsbury one. The Kingsman and ex-Captain of Boats, Robert Traill, left Moscow, where he was married to the daughter of the ex-War Minister of Kerensky's provisional government; he died at Brunete and his wife returned to Cambridge to live out the rest of her life. John Cornford declared that it was impossible to be a Communist and a pacifist; he left Trinity College for Spain, leaving behind him an unborn son and a Communist lover, Margot Heinemann; he was the first British volunteer in the Republican militia. His Christian name, which he did not use, was Rupert, given to him in memory of Rupert Brooke. He died trying vainly to defend the 'English Crest' at Cordoba. As he had written in his poem on the assassination of Kirov:

> Nothing is ever certain, nothing is ever safe,
> Today is overturning yesterday's settled good,
> Everything dying keeps a hungry grip on life.
> Nothing is born without screaming and blood...

At a memorial meeting in Cambridge, Michael Straight heard a Communist Party hack refer to Cornford as the finest type of middle-class comrade, as though he were not an individual. Current Party lessons were drawn from Cornford's death. His loss as a person was deeply felt by Straight and other friends such as Bernard Knox, a Classics scholar who had also gone to Spain, had been badly wounded and left for dead, and had returned to unemployment.

Another volunteer for the war, the Rhodes Scholar G.C.McLaurin, died at much the same time as Cornford. Because he had experience with a Maxim gun, Harry Pollitt had asked him to leave his Cambridge bookshop and to join the International Brigade, prompting an observation from the old Apostle F.L.Lucas that undergraduate pacifists often made good machine-gunners in Spain. These two Cambridge martyrs to a cause added to the political confusion in radical minds. At a memorial meeting, Aneurin

Bevan could declare to strong approval: 'John Cornford was a Communist and I am a member of the Labour Party. I believe that the sacrifice of Cornford, McLaurin and the International Brigade will weld the two parties into one.' And the President of the Cambridge Union could visit the Republican government in the Christmas vacation and simplify the complications of the struggle into the declaration that this was no war of Fascism against Communism, but a war of Fascism against the people.

Julian Bell was the first Apostle and son of Bloomsbury to die in the Civil War. He had left England to teach at Hankow University in China, which was preparing for an attack from the victorious Japanese armies in Manchuria. He returned to Cambridge, where he read a paper to the Apostles, renouncing pacifism and praising the military virtues. When his father and mother, Clive and Vanessa Bell, and other Bloomsberries tried to persuade him not to volunteer for the war, he told them it was too late for democracy and reason and persuasion and writing to the *New Statesman*. 'The only real choices are to submit or to fight.' In deference to his parents' beliefs, he went to Spain as an ambulance driver in the British Medical Unit of the International Brigades, but he was blown up by a bomb near Madrid in July 1937. Badly disfigured, he died near his friend from King's, Archibald Cochrane, a wealthy young natural scientist, who became head of the Medical Unit and its Madrid hospital. Cochrane survived to serve in the Second World War and have a distinguished career afterwards in medicine, but Julian Bell's death signalled the end of Bloomsbury itself.

Vanessa Bell's son had been as tall and handsome and outgoing as her beloved brother Thoby Stephen, who had introduced the Cambridge Apostles to his two sisters in London before his tragic early death in 1906. The influence of Bloomsbury with its emphasis on individual excellence had begun after Thoby's end. That influence had lasted for twenty years until the end of Julian Bell, who died for a mass cause and a collective ideology. In a time when Bell himself had declared that most intelligent young men were Marxist, the ideals of Bloomsbury appeared selfish and retrograde. The leaders of the old guard were already gone, Lytton Strachey and Roger Fry, and although some of the younger post-war associates such as George Rylands and Raymond Mortimer and Kenneth Clark carried on the artistic and personal attitudes of Bloomsbury, the times were out of joint. Even the significance of Virginia Woolf was hardly appreciated in the days when the Left Book Club appeared to be the messenger of the truths to come.

Pacifism was now at a discount. Like Julian Bell, the radicals were turning from the ideal of world peace to the need to fight Fascism, from disarmament to preparations to arm, if not actually fight in the Civil War. The leading young poet, Stephen Spender, was even recruited by Harry Pollitt as a correspondent for the *Daily Worker* and – if it might be – a martyr for the Party and the cause. It was W. H. Auden, however, who produced the best poem in English about the war, 'Spain 1937':

> What's your proposal? To build the Just City? I will.
> I agree. Or is it the suicide pact, the romantic
> > Death? Very well, I accept, for
> I am your choice, your decision: yes, I am Spain.

Auden did not suffer a romantic death as Julian Bell did, nor did he achieve what he predicted for 'to-morrow, for the young, the poets exploding like bombs'. He seemed like a gutless Kipling to George Orwell, who was actually fighting; Spender and the other middle-class writers on the fringe of the war were 'parlour bolsheviks'. Orwell's experiences, summed up in his *Homage to Catalonia*, were to make him an implacable enemy of Communism and its techniques for taking power; but he was not the only major writer who fought for the Republicans. The journalist Humphrey Slater, educated at private schools and the Slade School of Art, rose to be Chief of Operations of the International Brigades. His neglected novel, *The Heretics*, which compared the medieval Children's Crusade to the Spanish Civil War and was an indictment of fanaticism, was a major work. He himself was to turn from Communism during the Second World War to write another novel, *The Conspirator*, a savage attack on Soviet methods of recruiting, running and blackmailing secret agents. Its publisher, the Cambridge poet John Lehmann, considered that their friends, Guy Burgess and Donald Maclean, played out the story of the novel in actual life.

The Spanish Civil War was extremely useful to Stalin and the Soviet system in many ways. As the sole suppliers of war material to the Republican side, Russia appeared to be the supporter of a democratic government, fighting for its existence against totalitarian military rebels supplied by the Fascist powers, Italy and Germany. The battlegrounds in Spain were an opportunity to test armaments, real conditions involving real loss of life, the prelude to a certain war in the future between Bolshevism and Fascism. The Iberian conflict also drew attention from Stalin's genocide and purges in Russia, the killing and imprisonment of some five million Ukrainians for opposing forced collective farming, and the paranoid decimation of the Soviet military, bureaucracy and intelligentsia. Finally, the Popular Front and anti-Fascist policies of European radical opinion provided an opportunity to extend Soviet influence and covert activities among fellow-travellers everywhere.

In 1937, General Walter Krivitsky, who styled himself the head of Soviet military intelligence in Europe, defected to the west. He testified that the Comintern had spent most of its resources in Germany and in Central Europe during the nineteen-twenties. But with the rise of Fascism in the thirties, its funds were devoted to making European public opinion sympathetic to Stalin and to placing Soviet supporters in key positions in certain democratic governments. Its operational budget in France, Great Britain and the United States was very much increased. Two years previously, Stalin had addressed the Red Army training schools and had advocated the creation of cadres of Party enthusiasts willing to promote clandestinely the policies of the Seventh Communist International, which advocated a Popular Front and an alliance with European Social Democrats, the 'social Fascists' of yesteryear. This had led to many open Communists being instructed to go underground or even to change sides. Just as the best method of defence may be offence, so the best method of subversion may be jingoism or even officially aiding the enemy. Lenin himself had kept a known Tsarist agent on the Bolshevik Central Committee in order to reassure his opponents and feed them with false information.

At Cambridge, Guy Burgess was instructed to become a mole. After visiting Russia with a homosexual Communist friend from

Oxford, Derek Blaikie, and after meeting some of the heads of the Comintern, he suffered a flamboyant conversion to the virtues of Fascism, declaring that the National Socialism of Hitler and Mussolini was dialectically superior to the state capitalism of Stalin. He joined the Anglo-German Fellowship, visited Nazi Germany with a reactionary Conservative Member of Parliament, Captain Jack Macnamara, joined the talks department of the British Broadcasting Corporation where he was responsible for political reporting in 'The Week in Westminster', and made contact with a homosexual aristocratic German diplomat, Baron Wolfgang zu Puttlitz, a Junker who secretly opposed Hitler's aggressions. Such a volte-face in Burgess's beliefs seemed incredible to all his friends except those Communists who knew of his reasons for deserting them.

To most people, he was merely unstable. He did confess to one friend from Oxford, Goronwy Rees, that he was a Comintern agent and had been one ever since he had left Cambridge. The Party had told him to break off all communication with it as dramatically as possible, while continuing to serve its cause. His sense of theatre, of course, had made the break most dramatic. He asked Rees to help him in his work as a secret agent, but Rees chose not to believe Burgess, who might be playing a cruel joke on him. 'And even if he was sharing a secret, as he seemed to be doing, what trust could be placed in anything he said?' He even compromised the closed society of the Apostles. As the historian from King's, Sir Steven Runciman declared, the secrecy of the Apostles was much reduced when the left-wingers had more or less taken it over. Nobody could expect Burgess to be discreetly silent about anything, which made his later employment by the Foreign Office so extraordinary.

Donald Maclean was similarly instructed by Soviet intelligence. He could not join the Foreign Office unless he became a mole. When he was examined orally before admission, he was asked if he still held the strong Communist views which he had held at Cambridge. He decided to brazen it out with a show of honesty. 'I did have such views,' he declared, 'and I haven't entirely shaken them off.' He was accepted into the diplomatic service. When Harold Macmillan was later defending the government's decision to retain

Maclean in the diplomatic service for sixteen years until his defection, he asked the House of Commons whether Communist sympathies as an undergraduate should automatically exclude a man from public service. The Labour members shouted, 'No.' Some of them, including the future Minister of Defence, Denis Healey, had been Communist sympathizers as students. 'Surely it would have been regarded as one of the aberrations of youth,' Macmillan said of Maclean, 'which he might have been expected to live down.'

Maclean did not live down his Communist sympathies; he hid them. Kim Philby, too, was ordered to simulate a switch of allegiance. He had been an active Communist in Vienna during the purge by Dollfuss in 1934: he had even married a Party militant, Elisabeth Kohlmann, and had brought her back to England. He was also told to join the Anglo-German Fellowship. His apparent conversion convinced intelligent observers like Malcolm Muggeridge, to whom Philby confessed an admiration for Goebbels and a wish to work for his Nazi propaganda department. On the outbreak of the Spanish Civil War, however, Philby was sent to Spain as a Soviet intelligence agent, while apparently reporting favourably on Franco's forces for the English press. His job was to find out the extent of German involvement; arbitrarily arrested, he had to swallow the scrap of paper containing his code and cover addresses. This meaningless incident, he later reflected, put him in mortal hazard, while the real risk he took by being a Soviet agent was less dangerous, because he could take precautions and disguise himself.

Anthony Blunt, the fourth of the notorious Cambridge Soviet agents, was told to hide his ideology under his erudition at a later date. He was still an open Marxist during the Spanish Civil War. The painters promoted by Roger Fry and Bloomsbury, Van Gogh and Matisse, were the enemies of society in their pursuit of private vision. Contributing to Cecil Day Lewis's symposium, *The Mind in Chains*, Blunt made his ideology still more clear in an article on 'Art Under Capitalism and Socialism'. Impressionist painters had divorced the artist from the masses. The great painters of social realism were those of the Mexican Revolution, Orozco and Diego Rivera, who might be bourgeois, but were helping the

proletariat to produce its own culture. They were backed by the
state and approved by the masses. Even for artists, Blunt praised
Lenin's statement, 'We communists cannot stand with our hands
folded and let chaos develop in any direction it may. We must
guide this process according to a plan and form its results.' He
agreed with Lurçat's phrase: 'Art is no longer a free game; it is
an offensive activity.' As John Cornford had declared before his
death in Spain, 'The traditional artist's "impartiality" is unmasked
as a denial of the class struggle – as a powerful instrument in the
hands of the possessing classes.'

Such overt Marxist criticism made Blunt's ideology clear in the
mid-thirties. Before the outbreak of the Second World War, however, his views had gone underground. His art reviews became aus-
tere and scholarly, distinguished for their integrity and lack of
doctrine. He specialized in Poussin and the baroque, in Italian
painters and French architecture before the Revolution. Like other
Soviet agents, he was ordered to hide his political faith and infiltrate
the intelligence services. Before leaving Cambridge for the Warburg
Institute and London University, he recruited two more Soviet
agents among scholars at Trinity: the Apostle Leo Long, who was
to join MI14 and analyse German military movements, and John
Cairncross, who joined the diplomatic service before transferring
to the Treasury and then to the code-breakers at Bletchley Park,
who developed the ultimately war-winning process: breaking the
German Enigma-machine codes.

Another of Blunt's recruits was Michael Straight, who was told
to stage a breakdown after John Cornford's death, to cut all his
political ties, and prepare to work on Wall Street as an economic
spy. Stalin himself, Blunt declared, wanted Straight to take the
crooked way. Together, they met a Russian contact in a public
place off the Great West Road. The Russian agent told Straight
to telephone from booths, and he was given half of a torn piece
of paper, which would be matched when another Russian contact
approached him in America. The meeting was disappointing and
seedy. The Russian seemed to Straight more like the agent
of a small smuggling operation than the representative of a new
international order.

66

To Robert Cecil, a British diplomat for thirty years and a contemporary of the four Cambridge spies, the contest between Soviet intelligence and British counter-intelligence before the Second World War resembled a football match between Manchester United and the Corinthian Casuals, professionals against amateurs. The British MI5 had a small staff and few successes. In 1939, a spy ring was exposed passing secrets of naval armaments from the Woolwich Arsenal to the Russians. A Foreign Office cypher clerk, Captain John King, was also trapped after the defector Krivitsky's revelations: he had been recruited as a Soviet agent by Douglas Springhall. But the nascent 'Cambridge Comintern', so-called by Robert Cecil because its members could blinker themselves into believing that they were working for the international aims of Communism rather than directly for the Kremlin, was undetected as it infiltrated the diplomatic service and the media. Stalin would dissolve the Comintern in 1943; but by then, his foreign agents would be too implicated to extricate themselves by casuistry.

There was, however, no known 'Oxford Comintern'. Whether the older university was more discreet or less committed, history has not disclosed. What is certain is that it had no equivalent of the Apostles. Its congregation of the elect and the best was All Souls, its fellows known to all, even when they joined the civil service. Entry to that Oxford college of privilege may have been a sinecure, but it was never a conspiracy. All Souls flaunted its superiority without responsibility, but it was never clandestine, without accountability. The equivocal Goronwy Rees resigned from his fellowship there to go to Vienna and Berlin in 1933, where he 'played at conspiracy' with the remnants of the Austrian and German Communist Parties. Guy Burgess's attempt to recruit him as a Soviet agent appears to have been based on a greater Marxist commitment than Rees admits in his autobiographies. Certainly, Robert Cecil denounced Rees as a Soviet spy up to the time of the Stalin–Hitler Pact. Rees, however, was to serve bravely as a Territorial Army officer throughout the Second World War and was to give information to the British security services on Blunt and Burgess after the latter's defection. Rees accused Blunt of being a schizophrenic and a liar, and certainly a homosexual partner of Burgess, who pimped for him. In return, Blunt accused Rees of being a Soviet agent, tit for tat.

When he volunteered for the Territorial Army – an unlikely act which seemed criminal to many of his Oxford radical friends – Rees did not find himself alone. Other volunteers had once voted for the resolution of the Oxford Union in 1933, 'That this House will not fight for King and Country.' The change in their convictions was caused by Hitler and by Neville Chamberlain, who seemed the nightmare figures of the pre-war years – blood brothers, mirror images, *Doppelgänger*. Yet Rees still believed that all politics was underpinned by a reality variously called the working class or the masses or the proletariat. His beliefs were a curious hybrid of Marxism and Oxford idealism, just as Cambridge radicals espoused historical materialism crossed with G.E.Moore's doctrine of the value of personal relations. 'Perhaps even then we were unsure of our own muddle-headedness.' Yet Rees himself firmly believed he had in his possession 'the key to all the mysteries of existence'.

Prominent among the Oxford Communists was the extravagant Philip Toynbee, who was the organizing secretary of the university Party, although it only had a hundred permanent members with another hundred who threw away their cards as soon as they could. He exemplified the dandy Marxist, split between an aristocratic life-style and a romantic identification with the masses. Jessica Mitford, who had married Winston Churchill's nephew, Esmond Romilly, and had been collected by a British destroyer from the Basque zone of the Spanish Civil War, characterized Toynbee as an exuberant, overgrown, drunken puppy, and the only contact between the Communist Party and the estranged world of London society. Romilly himself refused to join the Party because he felt it was overloaded with young upper-class intellectuals and therefore unrealistic. There were too many Oxbridge graduates trying to purge themselves of the smell of class superiority through political extremism. Jessica Mitford noted how often Communists were expelled from the Party and turned against it, denouncing everything they had believed. Yet the Communists were the leaders in the fight against Fascism and unemployment, even if their internecine squabbles and internal dramas blunted their purpose. There were rather too many false theatricals attached to membership to suit those who had seen the awful disasters of the war in Spain.

Influential fellow-travellers, however, did come from Oxford, notably Tom Driberg, a homosexual journalist and later Socialist Member of Parliament, who became a friend and biographer of Guy Burgess, and served as a double agent for British and Russian intelligence. Claud Cockburn, a cousin of Evelyn Waugh, became a journalist, working first for *The Times*, then for the Communist *Daily Worker*, then founding his own newsletter, *The Week*, which was a radical political gossip sheet, the *Private Eye* of the thirties; its chief claim to fame was naming and exposing the pro-German appeasers of the 'Cliveden Set', politicians and men of influence who met at the Astors' country house. Cockburn decided he was with the Communists. He joined with them because he thought they were, in the main, right. He was certainly no liberal, to clash in battle against Hitler under banners inscribed 'On the one hand, on the other hand'.

The Spanish Civil War seemed to most radicals to be the prelude to a world war in which the Fascist powers would attack Russia, which might not be aided by the champions of non-intervention, France and Great Britain. As the Labour politician Sir Charles Trevelyan said: 'When the war that is looming comes and Japan and Germany crash in to destroy Soviet Russia, I hope the Labour Party will have some other policy to offer than sympathy, accompanied by bandages and cigarettes.' With the conflict very probable and the dogs of war let slip, the Comintern both cried havoc and directed its foreign sympathizers to become moles within their own governments and intelligence services. The skills of foreign scientists were needed to aid Russian industrialization and rearmament. They were the soldiers in the modern Trojan horse of invention, which might destroy the capitalist cities that dragged it within their walls.

The exodus of many of the leading Marxist undergraduates and dons from Cambridge in the thirties was matched by a similar departure of radical scientists. Patrick Blackett and Jack Haldane departed in 1933, Peter Kapitsa in 1934, Desmond Bernal three years later. Haldane went to University College London, which he declared was 'as full of bloody Communists as Cambridge'. He was, however, driven towards Marxism himself by hatred of the actions of Hitler and General Franco, and of the benevolent non-intervention of the British government. He decided to see the Spanish Civil War at first hand and went on three occasions to advise the Spanish government and the British Battalion of the International Brigades on how to resist possible gas attacks. His experiences turned him into one of the few British scientists to observe Fascist air raids on the cities of Madrid and Barcelona. On his return, he plunged into the Communist-backed 'Help Spain' and Air Raid Precautions movements which seemed to him necessary countermeasures against a likely Fascist attack.

To understand the attraction of Marxism to radical scientists of the period, *The Crisis in Physics* must be read. It was written by the young Christopher Caudwell, real name St. John Sprigg. He died on the Spanish front at Jarama; his work was edited and published posthumously by the Oxford Marxist, Professor Hyman Levy. Caudwell declared it was no accident that the crisis in physics was occurring at the same time as an unprecedented economic crisis. He quoted Planck's remark that every scientific axiom was now denied by somebody: every branch of western spiritual and material civilization was at a critical turning-point. Society was ravaged by wars, slumps, neuroses, unemployment and poverty, merely because men were ignorant of necessity. That knowledge of necessity, those inner laws of society and scientific progress were provided by belief in Marxism. True freedom was to submit to the laws of necessity, the dictates of the Communist Party.

In spite of later myths, few radical scientists went to fight for the Spanish Republic. They were outnumbered by writers in the British Battalion. One of the eleven commanders of the British Battalion in action was an industrial chemist, Bill Alexander; two were writers. David Haden-Guest, the leading mathematician and Marxist philosopher from Trinity College, Cambridge, volunteered and was killed at his observation post at the Ebro. The radical Oxford zoologist, Sir Peter Chalmers Mitchell, was living in Malaga and served as a contact between Soviet agents and the Spanish Communist Party. But it was practical workers from the mines and the factories, who supplied the mass of the two thousand seven hundred British combatants in the Spanish Civil War.

At home, the burgeoning Left Book Club brought together Communists and Socialists with those who opposed war and Fascism and unemployment. In it, the scientists' group was far the most active of the special occupational groups, attracting over three hundred people to its meetings, which were usually addressed by Bernal and Haldane. Michael Straight had first been influenced towards Marxism by Bernal, who declared he was a member of the Communist Party and was loudly cheered at a packed meeting of students at the London School of Economics. The Left Book Club published a series of radical classics such as the Webbs' *Soviet Communism: A New Civilization*; John Strachey's *The Coming Struggle for Power*, and Konni Zilliacus's *The Road to War*. The Club was ably organized by Strachey and Harold Laski and Victor Gollancz; it served as the microcosm of a British Popular Front, and its scientific members were the most influential part of it. Significantly, it would not publish Orwell's visceral attack on the Communist purge of other anarchist and Socialist groups in Spain, *Homage to Catalonia*. 'Gollancz', Orwell accused, 'is of course part of the Communism racket.'

Other book clubs also tackled the subjects of the day. Some idea of contemporary opinion can be found in a Book Club selection for 1938, the best-selling Dennis Wheatley's popular *Red Eagle, The Story of the Russian Revolution*. In that book, Wheatley denounced the sufferings which the Soviet system had brought on the people, but he expressed an admiration for Stalin and particularly for Marshal Voroshilov. He believed in the success of Stalin's Five-Year Plans in developing industry, communications and Siberia. Above all, he trusted Stalin's pacific intentions. The Soviet Union did not have the will or the capacity to declare war on the capitalist countries. Scientific Socialism was being achieved at a terrrible cost, but as an example to other nations, not as a threat.

Even to conservative thinkers and popular writers, national planning and the transformation of the world by the application of science appeared to be the future. Despite its shortcomings, the

Russian regime was building that future. Although the United States of America and some countries in Europe were technologically more advanced, the great depression had thrown tens of millions out of work and left the machines of the west running at half their capacity. In Soviet Russia, there seemed to be no unemployment. Even if working conditions were bad, everybody worked and was working for the benefit of the next generation. It was symptomatic that in May 1939, a poll of three thousand Cambridge students found three-quarters in favour of an alliance with Russia, while three-fifths were now in favour of conscription. The enemy was Fascism: there had been a sea-change in university thinking after the Spanish Civil War, Hitler's aggression against Czechoslovakia and his Pact of Steel with Mussolini.

The sea-change affected the radical scientific workers. The Anti-War Group lost influence. Many of the Marxist scientists were being recruited, along with the best minds at the Cavendish, into the preparations for a war against Fascism. Blackett was approached along with the physiologist A.V. Hill to sit on a Committee for the Scientific Study of Air Defence, set up under the chairmanship of the remarkable Oxford chemist Henry Tizard. It investigated the possibility of creating a death ray to counter air attacks, but decided that the detection of aircraft by radio waves was more practical. Against the advice of Winston Churchill's scientific adviser, F.A. Lindemann, who had expanded the Clarendon Laboratory at Oxford to be second only to the Cavendish in the study of physics, Tizard took the decision to develop radar and train the Air Force in its use before it had passed its trials. It was a choice, as Blackett pointed out, of doing something that might work as against doing nothing. By the time of the Battle of Britain, the radar stations were working well enough. They had a major, and perhaps decisive, effect on that battle.

Tizard was a good friend of Rutherford. By 1938, a number of Cavendish physicists had become advisers on radar. John Cockcroft was approached by Tizard, told of the secret radar stations, and asked to join the Committee of Air Defence. He informed Tizard of the cyclotrons being constructed at Cambridge and Liverpool for further experiments on splitting the atom. It was the same year that Otto Hahn successfully performed nuclear fission on the uranium atom in his Berlin laboratory. He gave his results to his German-Jewish colleague Lise Meitner, who had fled Germany for Niels Bohr's research institute in Copenhagen before moving on to Stockholm. Bohr informed western physicists of Hahn's discoveries, while Russian agents in Sweden relayed Meitner's information to Moscow and Abram Joffé, who had worked with Hahn and could interpret his formulae. At the same time, the Communist French scientist, Joliot-Curie, had made progress in achieving a chain-reaction after atomic fission. He put his results at the disposal of the Soviet Union for checking, but to be kept secret. With the use of a modified Wilson cloud chamber from the Cavendish and Mond Laboratories, two Russian researchers demonstrated the effects of short fission, the disintegration of a uranium nucleus under varied high-voltage bombardments. By the end of June 1939, the necessary theoretical research for the construction of a Soviet atomic bomb had been carried out, ten years before it became a practical device.

The major physicists in the east and the west knew of the potential weapon after Hahn had made his discovery. Most of the world's supply of uranium came from the Belgian Congo and some from Canada, although there were known deposits in Czechoslovakia and in Central Asia near Lake Ulungur. The only commercial producer of the 'heavy water' necessary for turning hydrogen into deuterium for the manufacture of another type of nuclear bomb was a Norwegian hydroelectric plant, in which the German chemicals firm I.G.Farben was involved. Conscious of the consequences if Hitler should acquire a nuclear bomb, Winston Churchill asked F.A.Lindemann to find out about its feasibility. A month before the outbreak of the Second World War, Churchill informed the British Air Minister that an atomic weapon could be manufactured within several years. He doubted, however, if Hitler would commit enough resources to make a nuclear bomb sooner. There was no need to be scared by the veiled threats of the German ambassador in London:

There are a lot of rumours going about this atomic explosive, and Ribbentrop has made remarks to people on the subject. I expect Lindemann's view is right, that there is no immediate danger, although undoubtedly the human race is crawling nearer to the point where it will be able to destroy itself completely.

C.P.Snow made the position clearer in an editorial in the scientific magazine *Discovery* written on the outbreak of the war. It was no secret that laboratories in the United States, Germany, France and England had been working feverishly on atomic fission for several months. If the manufacture of a bomb was practicable, science would have altered the scope of warfare. Scientists were losing hope. Even the invention of flight had been perverted to bomb human beings. As Snow declared:

> We cannot delude ourselves that this new invention will be better used. Yet it must be made, if it really is a physical possibility. If it is not made in America this year, it may be next year in Germany. There is no ethical problem; if the invention is not prevented by physical laws, it will certainly be carried out some-where in the world. It is better, at any rate, that America should have six months' start.
>
> But again, we must not pretend. Such an invention will never be kept secret; the physical principles are too obvious, and within a year every big laboratory on earth would have come to the same result. For a short time, perhaps, the U.S. Government may have this power entrusted to it; but soon after it will be in less civilized hands.

Snow did not mention Russia in his editorial, although he knew that Kapitsa and Joffé would certainly be directed to work on the atomic bomb at their institute in Moscow. In the Hitler war, as Snow foresaw, physicists would become the most essential of military resources. They would begin to be soldiers-not-in-uniform. They would have to be secret about their researches and findings. The years of the free flow of scientific data were finished. Exchanges of information had continued between the physicists of Cambridge and the Soviet Union even after Kapitsa's switch in 1934. Rutherford had given permission for three of Kapitsa's research assistants to join him in Moscow to work with him on his helium liquefier sent over from the Mond Laboratory. Cockcroft visited Kapitsa and his wife. His Moscow institute made fundamental discoveries in the superfluidity of liquid helium and became a major centre of atomic research with Lev Landau as its chief theoretical physicist. Yet Kapitsa regretted the freedom of research of his Cambridge days. 'What a wonderful time it was then at the Cavendish,' he lamented to an English friend. 'The science belonged to the scientists and not to the politicians.'

The death of Rutherford in 1937 signalled the end of an epoch for Kapitsa. As his sympathizer J.G.Crowther testified, it was for him the beginning of a new period in the history of human culture, characterized by the scientific-technological revolution. In his case, it was research in atomic energy. He could only hope that humanity would in the end use it beneficially. He had, however, no doubt that initially his research would be used by the Soviets to manufacture an atomic weapon in order to defend the homeland of the Russian Revolution. What he had once written of Rutherford, he could write of his new overlord, Stalin: 'His moods fluctuate violently. It will need great vigilance if I am going to obtain, and keep, his high opinion.'

Kapitsa threw all his gifts into his new atomic work and the cause of Soviet science. 'It was only then that we, who had known him in Cambridge,' C.P.Snow wrote, 'realised how strong a character he was: how brave he was and fundamentally what a good man.' His courage was shown in his actions in saving dozens of Jewish scientists from the Stalinist show trials and purges of 1937 to 1939, when any possible foreign allegiance was considered a conspiracy against the state. The brilliant Lev Landau, who would win the Nobel Prize for his research as Kapitsa did himself, was put in prison as a German spy. Kapitsa personally intervened with Stalin and stated that all atomic research work would stop until Landau was released. His boldness won over Stalin, although it could have earned a death sentence. Landau was freed along with other necessary scientists, whose power of subversion was certainly less than their use to the state. Kapitsa was of such great use himself that he was never prosecuted for his foreign contacts. 'Through him', Snow testified later in *The Moral Un-Neutrality of Science*, 'a generation of English scientists came to have personal knowledge of their Russian colleagues. These exchanges were then, and have remained, more valuable than all the diplomatic exchanges ever invented.'

In spite of official denials and disinformation, Kapitsa's role in nuclear research has been disclosed. He was the leader of a distinguished group of Russian atomic physicists, which included N.K.Semyonov, D.D.Ivanenko and G.N.Tamm. He was given the power of recruiting six hundred assistants for his new research institutes: many of them were rescued from Siberian camps. The money spent on the recruitment in three weeks, Kapitsa told Joffé, would have kept the Cavendish going for a good year. Two committees were formed from leading members of the Academy of Sciences, a physics board which included Joffé, Krylov, S.I.Vavilov, and I.V.Kurchatov, a pioneer of nuclear research whom Kapitsa had released from the Lubyanka prison; and a metallurgical board led by leading Soviet specialists: Kapitsa himself was the only scientist serving on both boards. Atomic research centres were installed at Lake Van, Baykal-Angara, and Karaganda-Semipalatinsk, the first three of nine such centres. Massive state funds were committed for their construction, as also for the manufacture of a large cyclotron in Leningrad, based on drawings and plans for the largest one in the world at Berkeley, California: these American blueprints were passed on to Moscow by Soviet agents in America. In fact, an atomic espionage section was formed within Russian intelligence on the principle that it was better to benefit from other countries' research than to develop only one's own.

Russian atomic research was split into two units: a fission unit led by Kurchatov and a fusion unit led by Kapitsa, whose particular study was low-temperature work on helium and hydrogen. As early as the summer of 1940, Kapitsa spoke at a physics conference in Moscow, predicting the release of huge reserves of energy from liquid hydrogen processed into deuterium and tritium, 'heavy' hydrogen made in uranium piles. The formation of an atomic committee in the Kremlin under Stalin himself, and the commitment of more and more resources to the development of nuclear weapons in order to stay in advance of German and American research, led to significant Russian advances in the field. By New Year's Eve, 1941, Joffé could boast of a cyclotron large enough to smash the atomic nucleus and of fission research advanced enough to separate the uranium isotope 235 and to provide an ignition process for a bomb. In point of fact, plans for the best atomic trigger would be provided by Klaus Fuchs from abroad as a personal contribution to the Soviet war effort and the Communist cause.

Atomic espionage had to be organized by the Soviet state because the pre-war exchange of scientific research between European and Russian physicists could hardly survive the signing of the Stalin–Hitler Non-Aggression Pact, leading to the invasion and partition of Poland and the outbreak of the Second World War. The pact meant that scientific and atomic secrets passed to Moscow might be passed on to Berlin. The old basis of trust had gone. The Kapitsa phenomenon, as C.P.Snow recognized, could not take place again. 'After the idyllic years of world science,' he wrote, 'we passed into a tempest of history, and, by an unfortunate coincidence, we passed into a technological tempest too. The discovery of atomic fission broke up the world of international physics.'

The death of Lord Rutherford had already signalled the break-up of that world. Yet his teaching and his students helped to win the war against Fascism. As Cockcroft said after victory was won and he had been put in charge of a programme to develop British nuclear weapons:

Although Rutherford died in 1937, his influence was a major factor in the scientific supremacy of Britain in the war. The Senior Staff and research of the laboratory, together with members of other physics schools, were mobilized in the first days of the war and developed for Britain and the allied cause the centimetre radar which turned the tide of the U-boat battle, directed the bombing of Germany and helped decisively to sink the Japanese fleet. The Liverpool branch of the Rutherford School, with Frisch and Peierls from Birmingham, initiated the work on the atomic bomb which ended the war with Japan. One can only wish that Rutherford had been alive to deal with its consequences.

Rutherford departed almost like a Greek hero, in J.G.Crowther's opinion: he was taken into heaven at the summit of his glory, so that he was not alive to see his victories bartered away. He came from a simpler and healthier society. He would never have approved of how corruptly his successors used the discoveries to which he had contributed so much. He had freely helped Peter Kapitsa take a knowledge of theoretical and practical physics gained in a capitalist laboratory back to Soviet Russia along with the laboratory itself. There was no need for moles among scientists during the age of Rutherford. They worked wherever they could.

6 The Crisis of Commitment

The coming of the war saw some of the poets, philosophers and writers decide to slouch it out in the United States of America: Bertrand Russell, W.H.Auden and Christopher Isherwood. They were bitterly attacked for their decision. For those who stayed, such as Stephen Spender and John Lehmann, there was a crisis of faith because of the Nazi–Soviet pact. As Lehmann recorded, a huge hole was blown through the myth of an idealistic revolutionary Russia leading the forces of resistance to Hitler. Although there was a new party line that the war against Germany was now an imperialist war, it was farcical claptrap, even for committed comrades.

> What fanatical twist in their minds made it possible for them to accept the topsy-turvy reasoning that found it suddenly respectable to shake hands with the Jew-baiters, the murderers of Guernica, the plunderers of Austria and Czechoslovakia? Certainly they got little or no support from the people whose interests they were supposed to be defending.

Lehmann had endless discussions with Spender and many other fellow-travellers associated with them in the anti-Fascist and pro-Communist causes of the 1930s. They felt betrayed; all that they had done for peace and the Spanish Republic seemed meaningless. They justified themselves as humanists, who had spoken out for truth, even if clustered under a false red banner:

> Nothing that had happened made us feel that we had been wrong to stand openly for the ideas of liberty and justice, to show that we stood on the side of those parties and groups that appeared

79

to be championing them most effectively in the political struggles of a political decade. Our general position, we still felt, had been right: poets and other creative artists cannot, if they are to remain fully living people, if they are to fulfil their function as interpreters of their time to their own generation, fail to interest themselves in the meaning behind political ideas and political power. It was our particular position that had probably been wrong: in the heat of the battle, to give our specific assent to a particular set of slogans, even if we did not actually join a particular party.

For the Communist Party of Great Britain, the Nazi–Soviet pact was catastrophic. Its increase in Party members and sympathizers had been brought about by the fight against Fascism. Now Stalin was Hitler's ally. Harry Pollitt persuaded his Central Committee that in spite of the pact, the British Communists should still support a just war against Fascism, while campaigning for the removal of Chamberlain and the 'guilty men of Munich' who had appeased Hitler and sought to encourage him to attack Russia. Pollitt issued a pamphlet, *How To Win the War*, which was hurriedly withdrawn after Douglas Springhall returned from Moscow with instructions from the Communist International about the new line to be taken by fraternal Communist Parties. After the Nazi–Soviet pact, the war between the Axis and the Allied powers was to be seen as a war between imperialist rivals. There was no difference between a Fascist state and a bourgeois democracy, which was mere social Fascism. The policy to be pursued in Britain was, in Lenin's and Palme Dutt's elegant phrase, 'revolutionary defeatism'.

To Pollitt's credit, he spoke against the new policy imposed by Moscow. He said it would do very grave harm to the Party; he did not envy the comrades who could so lightly in the space of a week go from one political conviction to another. He was outvoted by the Central Committee and persuaded to recant in order to preserve Party unity. He had to think of the Russian action in making a pact with the Nazis, in Winston Churchill's terms, as a riddle wrapped in a mystery inside an enigma. There was perhaps a key, as Churchill suggested: that key was Russian national interest. But it was not British interest. Even for a Communist, to fight

80

Fascism from home and to support Fascism's Russian ally was more than a double loyalty could take. A terrible political isolation was imposed on the Communists in the first two years of the war. They were called Communazis. As the secret clauses in the Nazi–Soviet Pact were revealed – that Russia would supply oil and grain to Germany and exchange refugee German Communists for captured Russian agents – so that terrible isolation grew. It was possible to explain the Soviet snatch of eastern Poland as a move to preserve the land from Nazi occupation, but it was harder to excuse the swallowing of the small Baltic states and the assault on Finland. Until Hitler broke the pact and attacked Russia, the Communist Party had little to offer a patriotic nation fighting a foul ideology that was an anathema to most Communists themselves.

Arthur Koestler has written of the sin of the radical scientists during the Stalin–Hilter Pact. Among the hundreds of refugee Communists and Jews handed by the Russian secret police back to the Gestapo were the physicists Alex Weissberg and Fiesl Hautermans, who had been an assistant to Patrick Blackett. Blackett did protest about the Hautermans case to Moscow, but he refused to sign a cable to Stalin in defence of Weissberg, although it was signed by the three French physicists who were Nobel Prize winners, Perrin, Langevin and Joliot-Curie. The moral of the incident was clear to Koestler, that Joliot-Curie, Blackett and the rest of the 'nuclear Marxists' could not claim ignorance of what was happening in Russia. They knew the case histories of at least two of their colleagues who were loyal to the Soviet Union, yet arrested on grotesque charges, imprisoned for years without trial, then handed over to the Nazis. There were thousands of other known cases of false charges and long imprisonment among academics in Russia, particularly scientists. Among these were the biophysicist A.Chizhevsky, the biologists E.Kreps and A.Baev, and even the aeroplane designer Andrey Tupolev and the rocket expert Aleksey Korolev. These were the ones that Peter Kapitsa could not redeem, and western Marxist intellectuals chose to forget.

The apostasy of the pact convinced many Communists to leave the Party during the two years of its duration. Those who remained Communists constructed an apology which helped to explain why so many Soviet agents or 'moles' remained faithful during a time when secrets passed to the Comintern might well have been passed on to the Third Reich. After the fall of France, at the time that German armies were preparing for the invasion of Britain, information fed by Communists to Russia might be relayed to those invasion forces. Yet all was excusable, if the defence of the Soviet Union was paramount.

In a remarkable session of historical analysis forty years later, the British Communist Party examined its actions and feelings during the two years of the pact. The important thing was that Stalin's Soviet Union had to survive. It was the only hope for world Communism. 'Good old Joe,' one party member thought, 'the old fox has slipped out of the trap – he has avoided being isolated and left it to the imperialist rivals.' Another testified to the need for self-surrender, to fight for the party line as a good soldier should, not in the front line as a good British soldier should. Russia must survive. Russia was always right. The defence of Russia was more important than the defence of Britain.

Those who remained in the party were euphoric about the Non-Aggression Pact and the probable collapse of Britain and France. Michael Straight found his Communist friends believing that Stalin had fooled an anti-Soviet conspiracy, that the capitalist nations had blundered into war against each other, and that the war would lead to mutinies and riots which would culminate in a world revolution. Douglas Hyde, who was to defect from the party after the war, testified that the disaster of Dunkirk and the almost inevitable defeat of Britain seemed a magnificent opportunity to those who remained in the Communist Party.

> Taking this to heart we administered all the blows we could, through the tactic of the People's Convention, through trying to create war-weariness, through industrial disputes, through the spread of disaffection among members of the armed forces and through exploiting every possible grievance, political, social, economic or industrial, upon which we could seize.

At Cambridge, some of the Apostles who had been sympathizers now gloated at the discomfort of the Communists and their change of policy. In October 1939, John Maynard Keynes wrote to the *New Statesman*:

The intelligentsia of the Left were the loudest in demanding that the Nazi aggression should be resisted at all costs; when it comes to a showdown, scarce four weeks have passed before they remember that they are pacifists and write defeatist letters to your columns, leaving the defence of freedom to Colonel Blimp and the Old School Tie, for whom three cheers.

The truth was that a divided British cabinet and a lukewarm French administration had decided to seek an alliance with Russia too late. Poland could not be defended from a German attack without Russian aid, and a guarantee had been given to Poland. The British Prime Minister Chamberlain had opposed a Soviet alliance, thinking that it would provoke Hitler into war, but he had finally accepted the principle of a triple pact very reluctantly and very disturbed by its implications. A British military mission had been sent by slow boat to Leningrad in August 1939, where it had begun discussions on combined operations with French and Russian representatives. Simultaneously, Stalin had been negotiating his pact with Hitler; his Foreign Minister Molotov had signed it with Ribbentrop on 23 August, eight days before the German attack on Poland that led to its partition with the Russians. While the Soviet agreement with its Nazi enemy may have temporarily helped the cause of national preservation, Stalin had rebuffed the democratic powers, destroyed all illusions that Russia was the champion of anti-Fascism, and betrayed the beliefs of many of the Communists who had joined the Party in the heady and hopeful middle years of the decade.

Nothing hurt the Soviet position more than its unprovoked attack on democratic Finland in 1940 soon after it had swallowed up the Baltic states. The war was covered by a British war correspondent, John Langdon-Davies, whose dispatches from the Spanish Civil War had praised Russian support of the Republicans and had attacked Fascist aid to the rebels under Franco. He went to Finland with various assumptions. He refused to believe Stalin's methods

of warfare could be indistinguishable from those of Hitler and
Mussolini, or of the Tsar. How could a government, after twenty-
three years of the dictatorship of the proletariat, 'willingly sacrifice
human life with a liberality usually attributed only to profit-making
merchants of death?' But he saw the Red Army disintegrate into
hordes of recruits sent in waves against the Finnish machine-guns.
It was a brilliant defence of a homeland fought by a small people
against a greater aggressor, in which the Finns slaughtered their
enemies and destroyed the myths of Russian liberation. Although
ruthlessly defeated in the end, Finland was not defeated by treason
and fifth columns. 'That is her great claim to glory in the eyes
of a rotten world.'

Only small parts of the social world were rotten in England,
where a fifth column was unimportant. For those who were already
Russian agents, the outbreak of the war presented an incentive
to change jobs rather than an opportunity for confession. Although
Guy Burgess later claimed to have had doubts about his Soviet
allegiance during the Stalin–Hitler Pact, he temporarily resigned
from his broadcasting job to join Section D of MI6 of the Secret
Intelligence Service, which was set up to organize propaganda and
sabotage abroad; it was so small that its London staff could fit
into a large drawing-room. At one point, Burgess arranged to
accompany the Oxford don Isaiah Berlin to Moscow to assist the
new ambassador there, Sir Stafford Cripps, but his mission was
aborted at the last moment. He was able to prove, however, his
worth as a British agent. His Soviet contacts had instructed him
to keep under surveillance the activities of White Russian émigrés
in London; so he was able to denounce Anna Volkov, the secretary
of a pro-German organization called the Right Club. Her friend
was a young cypher clerk in the American embassy, Tyler Gatewood
Kent, who photographed and passed on to Volkov hundreds of
confidential messages between Winston Churchill, then First Lord
of the Admiralty, and Franklin D. Roosevelt. According to Kent,
the president of the United States was conspiring with Churchill
to make him Prime Minister and to bring America into the conflict
in Europe. Kent claimed that he only intended to leak the documents
to the American press, in order to prove that Roosevelt was deceiv-

ing the American public and wanted to intervene in the war on the British side. His lover Volkov, however, was giving the messages to the Italian embassy, which was transmitting them to Germany. As the American ambassador in London, Joseph Kennedy, declared, Kent's treachery and betrayal of the codes and cyphers blacked out all American diplomatic communications at a most terrible moment in history: soon after Dunkirk and the fall of France.

This espionage *coup* made Burgess *persona grata* in British intelligence circles. Although he himself had to return to his broadcasting work after the break-up of Section D during a reorganization, he remained on intimate terms with many leading figures in the world of covert operations. Through his Cambridge friend Victor Rothschild, one of the few scientific Apostles and an anti-sabotage expert for MI5 during the war, Burgess had become a financial adviser to Victor's mother on a generous monthly retainer – a fact that he gave as an explanation for the large sums of banknotes usually in his pockets. Victor Rothschild lent him a house at 5 Bentinck Street, which Burgess shared for a time with Anthony Blunt. It was the scene of drunken homosexual orgies and compromising situations that were the stuff of blackmail. In Malcolm Muggeridge's opinion, this millionaire's nest sheltered 'a whole revolutionary *Who's Who*', including the Communist scientist Desmond Bernal, engaged in planning for Combined Operations. The more significant regular visitors to Bentinck Street were Guy Liddell, a leading light in MI5, and Desmond Vesey from MI6, as well as Kim Philby and Donald Maclean. Liddell was mainly responsible for anti-Communist surveillance, but he became a close friend of Burgess and Blunt and Philby, who boasted of cultivating MI5 assiduously and of his many personal friends in the department.

Philby had achieved a role in intelligence with difficulty. Ironically, he had been excluded for the wrong reasons. His work for the Anglo-German Fellowship, his pro-Franco reporting from Spain, and his father's brief internment as a Fascist supporter, had made him seem a security threat as a crypto-Nazi. He was tarred by his own cover and parent. But after Burgess had procured his admission into Section D of MI6, he was promoted through a school for training special agents into the new Special Operations Executive, responsible for wartime sabotage and subversion. Its aim, in Churchill's words, was to set Europe ablaze. It did not, to Philby's disgust, because it would not use revolutionary propaganda. The *status quo* was to be preserved after the war.

By this time, Philby was a professional officer in the Soviet intelligence service. His reason for accepting the position was not ideological; it displayed the arrogance of the Englishman born to rule. 'When the proposition was made to me,' he wrote, 'I did not hesitate. One does not look twice at an offer of enrolment in an élite force.' The novelist Graham Greene, who served under Philby during the war, defended him for working, in his own eyes, for a shape of things to come from which his country would benefit. This was the treachery of a fanatic who had a chilling certainty in his own correct judgement.

But it was also the treason of English superiority, the inverted logic of inheritance. If a young man was denied a large immediate place in his own system, then he must work for others in order to achieve it for himself. Not for Philby the weaknesses of the Koestlers and the Muggeridges, who changed into querulous outcasts from Communism because of the brutalities of Stalin and the betrayal of the Nazi–Soviet Pact. Their views were petulant and personal, railing at the movement that had let them down, the god that had failed them. Philby stayed the course, in return quoting Greene from his novel *The Confidential Agent*: 'You choose your side once and for all – of course, it may be the wrong side. Only history can tell that.'

Other Russian agents from Cambridge achieved their aims. Anthony Blunt was finally accepted by MI5. One of his tasks was to survey the activities of the various European governments-in-exile in London. This information was extremely useful to Blunt's Soviet control, because the identities and policies of returned democratic leaders were to be of lethal use after the war to the pro-Russian governments installed in eastern Europe behind the advance of the Red Army. Blunt also inquired into the activities of Tsarist refugees in London. They were to suffer from his intelligence; thousands of them were returned to die in Russia in 1945 by the terms of the Yalta accords, which did not cover their case. He also became an expert in the rifling of diplomatic bags, the copying of their contents and their return without detection. It was easier than detecting the forgery of a work of art.

Meanwhile, Donald Maclean married in 1940 an American woman, Melinda Marling, and fathered two sons. His rise through the Foreign Office was steady and unspectacular, paving the way to an important appointment at the British embassy in Washington four years later. In Cyril Connolly's words, while Guy Burgess belonged to the febrile wartime café-society of the temporary civil servant, Maclean belonged to the secret citadel of the permanent. His occasional forays with Burgess into the *louche* quarters of Bentinck Street or Soho were discreet, unlike those of the decadent Brian Howard, who had managed through Burgess to join MI5, but was dismissed in 1942 for disclosing secrets to all the delectable youth and the walls with ears in the Gargoyle or the Ritz bar in his inescapable, affected whine. Quentin Crisp in *The Naked Civil Servant* may have described how he was so blatant a homosexual that he was made totally exempt from serving his country because he suffered from sexual perversion; but such obvious characteristics did not stop MI5 from employing a Burgess or a Howard, who seemed like Crisp more to glory in their deviance than suffer from it.

The selection of recruits to British intelligence was often by chance, if not by crony. Dennis Brogan, the Cambridge historian of France and the United States, was chosen to find agents to be sent to occupied France. There were two contradictory methods: only to send over experts in espionage – and few of these existed – or to send over nearly every volunteer who wished to go. Brogan chose the second principle. Unlikely and extravagant agents who knew little and could betray less might achieve great results from their very improbability. Their frequent capture by the Germans certainly seemd to show Allied incompetence and hid the skilled work of the undisclosed professionals among them. It was spying by scattershot, open to all who loved the risk. Initial recruitment to MI5 seems to have operated on the same principle, an opportunity open to any fantasist and would-be player of the great game, as long as he or she came from the right family or school or club or secret society. To have been a Marxist or a homosexual was no disqualification; to have the right connections and striped tie was to share the assumptions and personal honour of a ruling class. The roguish, elegant world of Evelyn Waugh's and Anthony Powell's novels reflected accurately the extraordinary expansion of the British intelligence services in the first years of the war. Security clearance was then hardly a necessity for an Old Etonian or a Cambridge Apostle, and Guy Burgess was both.

His flaunted indiscretions were, indeed, part of his cover. 'Until the day of his disappearance', Harold Macmillan asserted in the House of Commons, 'there were no grounds for suspecting that he was working against the security of the State. He had been indiscreet, but then indiscretion is not generally the characteristic of a secret agent.' It was Burgess's shocking style of life and reckless statements that prevented anyone from believing that he was a Soviet agent. Also, it was the excellence of his contacts and his peerless background. He was even mentioned in July 1940, in the correspondence of Sir Edward Marsh, the aesthete and sometime private secretary to Winston Churchill. Marsh, indeed, introduced Burgess to Churchill, who dedicated a book to him, an act which Burgess was to exploit all his life. Marsh wrote:

> I've had one outing – to dine on Saturday with the Cambridge Apostles (a Secret Society, one isn't supposed to mention its doings, but never mind). It was at the Ivy. I sat next a very attractive youth called Guy Burgess, working in MI6, most intelligent and 'live-wire'. He talked most of the time to E.M.Forster whom he had planned to sit next. Most of my talk was with Desmond MacCarthy and Bob Trevelyan, and J.T.Sheppard opposite – quite good, but I don't find I brought anything away.

Burgess brought away information wherever he chose to move, and he moved in the most important circles. Even when he issued his *apologia* in Moscow after his disappearance with Donald Maclean, he confessed that he had deliberately sought out those in great places in order to pursue his policies.

> At Cambridge [the public statement of the two defectors declared], we had both been Communists. We abandoned our

political activities not because we in any way disagreed with the Marxist analysis of the situation in which we still both find ourselves, but because we thought, wrongly it is now clear to us, that in the public service we could do more to put those ideas into practical effect than elsewhere.

That they chose or were instructed to choose to aim high and remain clandestine did not affect their commitment to their cause and the duties imposed on them. Even during the Nazi–Soviet Pact, when Maclean himself had to flee from the embassy in Paris with his new wife to escape falling into the hands of the advancing German armies, neither he nor Burgess appears to have doubted the rightness of their ideology or its eventual success. At a time when the weaknesses of the democracies seemed to have encouraged the attacks of Fascism, the very excesses, bloodthirstiness and ruthless diplomacy of Stalin were an encouragement to those who were too committed to Communism to be able to change or disbelieve. It was, as Graham Greene was to state in *The Comedians*, a faith that could not be abandoned without abandoning all faith. 'Communists have committed great crimes, but at least they have not stood aside, like an established society, and been indifferent.' With Doctor Magiot, Burgess and Blunt, Philby and Maclean could declare, 'I would rather have blood on my hands than water, like Pilate.'

Yet the Nazi–Soviet Pact did drive away from Communism many of its members in the thirties. John Strachey, who also lived for a time with Burgess in the house in Bentinck Street, left the Party. He sold his Russian bonds, bought stocks in General Motors, and sent his wife and children to Canada for safety during the blitz. Although he spent some Bohemian wartime months with his raffish London friends, he joined the Air Ministry. According to Goronwy Rees, if Bomber Command could have eavesdropped on some of the political intrigues that Strachey indulged in with Burgess and his associates, he would have been courtmartialled. However that was, Strachey gave up writing pro-Soviet propaganda. It was not Marxism that inspired his patriotic essay, 'A Faith to Fight For'. War was the great leveller. It even levelled the class war into a common war against Fascism for traditional values.

As in the First World War, the coming of the Second spread a bushfire of patriotism across the major universities. At Cambridge, dons and scientists were recruited by their hundreds for intelligence activities and scientific research for the war ministries. Known Communists were not barred from working on defence matters. Churchill himself, once he had taken over from Chamberlain as Prime Minister, decreed that Communists might work in all branches except in the intelligence services. As it was, the cryptographers and code-breakers at Bletchley numbered two dozen Cambridge dons, of whom thirteen came from King's College, including three members of the Apostles. Alan Hodgkin worked on radar while attached to the Air Ministry. Alister Watson also made great contributions to radar research as a government scientist in the Admiralty. David Champernowne was recruited by Churchill's scientific adviser F.A.-Lindemann to serve as a statistician for Churchill producing the tables and diagrams needed to control war production.

Outside the Apostles, other radical scientists who had been at Cambridge aided the war effort. Blackett designed a bomb-sight and collected a circus of young scientists around him to advise anti-aircraft headquarters on the best use of radar. Bernal was employed as a scientific adviser by the Ministry of Home Security and by Bomber Command. Haldane worked on physiological problems for the Royal Navy, using four ex-members of the International Brigades in submarine experiments. He continued tirelessly to lecture for the new Communist policy and joined the Party officially in 1942, causing his wife to leave him. She had noticed on a trip to Russia two years before how much things had changed since 1928. The élite then had been scientists, engineers, and skilled factory workers; now it tended to be bureaucrats and secret policemen.

After 1939, there were no discoveries of Russian agents in Britain during the two years of the Nazi–Soviet Pact. There was, however, the conviction of a member of the Communist Party of Great Britain, a merchant seaman called George Armstrong, for spying on Atlantic convoy movements from ports in the United States. Armstrong had been influenced by a speech made by the Soviet Foreign Minister Molotov soon after the Pact, when he had denounced the war of the Allies against the Axis powers as a capitalist plot directed at the working classes. He recommended that all workers should strike at munitions factories and dockers should refuse to load war materials. Armstrong took the speech at its face value, jumped ship at Boston, and offered his help to the German embassy in revealing ship movements to England. Less sophisticated than a Blunt or a Burgess, he presumed the Nazi–Soviet Pact meant the supply of secret information to the Germans directly, even if their armies stood opposite the white cliffs of Dover, ready to invade after Dunkirk. He was arrested, deported to his home country, tried in secret, and hanged after Hitler's attack on Russia. He had believed Molotov's speech only too literally, but when the Russians swung to outright support of the Allies – now their allies against Germany – it was too late to save his neck.

There was also in 1940 the strange case of Tyler Kent with his betrayal of the secret messages between Roosevelt and Churchill. He was not sentenced to the rope's end, but to seven years in prison. Almost certainly, he exaggerated the importance of the clandestine correspondence, which merely proved that the American navy was co-operating with the British navy in giving intelligence on the position of German ships, thus violating neutrality. Roosevelt's overt help to Britain was far more significant, the trading of fifty old American destroyers for bases in the West Indies, more stringent procedures for convoys, joint staff meetings, and orders to American warships to shoot on sight in the Atlantic. These measures led to an undeclared sea-war against Germany, before the Japanese attack on Pearl Harbor provoked an American intervention on the Allied side.

Although the English government did imprison an American embassy clerk for spying, it was prepared voluntarily to give the United States details of scientific advances in military areas. Tizard and Cockcroft sailed to America with a black japanned trunk full of Britain's newest secret developments. The most important was a cavity magnetron for generating intense, short-wavelength radio beams; it vastly improved the performance of British radar. There were also naval predictors and fire-control mechanisms, new bomb-sights and proximity fuses. The Americans were given these military secrets so that they could manufacture them and ship them back across the Atlantic, keeping some for their own rearmament programme. Most important of all, Cockcroft brought with him a three-page memorandum written by the refugee physicists, Rudolph Peierls and O.R.Frisch, working with Mark Oliphant at Birmingham. The memorandum correctly set down the requirements for manufacturing a small fission bomb. It was to serve as the basis for the gigantic Manhattan Project run by J.Robert Oppenheimer at Los Alamos, which was to produce the first atomic bombs five years later.

This open revelation of military technology to a foreign power, albeit the United States, was sanctioned by Churchill. He wished to involve America more in British war processes and to show how much Britain trusted its special relationship with the United States. It was in sharp contrast to his treatment of scientists who might pass military secrets to other neutral powers and the Soviet Union. Although Bernal and other known Communists were used on operational research, they were watched by the security services. The Communist newspaper, the *Daily Worker*, was suppressed for printing material against the war, and leading Communists were kept under surveillance. Some refugee scientists suspected of being Communist sympathizers were interned, for example, Hans Kahle and Klaus Fuchs, but both were released to work on research projects, Fuchs with Peierls on the development of an atomic bomb. From 1941 onwards, Fuchs directly supplied the Soviet embassy in London with full details of all British research work on nuclear weapons. His activities were not discovered for another eight years. He was one of at least twelve scientists in Canada, America and Britain who passed on to Soviet sources nuclear secrets and classified information during the Second World War.

When Hitler, however, attacked Russia in the summer of 1941, Cockcroft was keen to interchange nuclear and scientific information with the Russians, who had joined the Allied powers. On his own initiative, he sent out a telegram in October to the Russian Academy of Sciences during the Battle for Moscow:

Greetings to Russian scientists and especially to Kapitsa and my other friends in Russia who have worked with us in the past. Since the war began British scientists have devoted their entire energies to defeating the Nazi menace. We have for a year now been powerfully reinforced by the scientists of North America. With the further help of our Russian friends we will demonstrate that world science mobilised with a single objective can be one of the decisive factors in defeating the Hitler objective of a Nazi-controlled world slave state.

Cockcroft wished openly to exchange information, particularly on nuclear physics, with Kapitsa and the Russians, especially as these were now allies in the fight against the Fascist powers. Kapitsa responded with enthusiasm to the idea of co-operation between the wartime allies on the making of an atomic bomb; but Winston Churchill would not allow the flow of such information to the Russians, only to the Americans. Peierls and Frisch were both suspected of Communist sympathies and, despite their pioneer work on nuclear fission, they were not made members of the small MAUD committee which was responsible for work on a British nuclear bomb.

Cockcroft was to be chosen to organize and lead that atomic research work in Canada. Although he continued to press for sharing discoveries with the Russians, and although there was discussion in the War Cabinet about sending a mission to Moscow to promote the interchange of scientific and technical information directly connected with the war, that mission was indefinitely postponed in July 1943. Kapitsa was also pressing in Moscow for a conference of all leading physicists, Russian and British and American and European, including Planck and Oppenheimer and Einstein himself, to try and establish international controls on nuclear research among the Allied powers, and to regulate the production of the weapons of mass destruction. His letters to other leading physicists were suppressed. His work, particularly in atomic aggregates, continued. Russia exploded its first crude experimental device in September 1943, reportedly killing the assistant of Kurchatov who ignited it.

The collapse of the attempt to exchange data connected with

the war was partly due to an act of stupidity by Russian intelligence, working through Douglas Springhall, the emissary from Moscow who had caused the change in the British Party line in 1939. He was the national organizer for the Party at home; but he was also a hidden spymaster for the Comintern, recruiting agents such as Alexander Foote during his time as political commissar with the British Battalion in Spain. As Foote testified after leaving the Party in his *Handbook for Spies*, Springhall directly approached him to perform certain missions for the Red Army. Foote's motives were as confused as those of the fellow-travellers of the thirties. He did not become a Russian agent for money or for patriotism, nor was his idealism the primary cause:

> It was some time before I realised for whom I was working. Many conversations that I have had since with others who were 'in the net' have shown that they, too, at first had little idea – if any – of the identity of their masters, save that it was for the Communist ideal as a whole, which is, after all, the vaguest sort of master to have. In my case I was recruited out of the dark into the dark – a sort of blind catch-as-catch-can – and went into the arena of international espionage with my eyes open, but open under a black bandage. I knew that I was a spy and knew against whom I was supposed to be spying, but at first had no idea of the why and wherefore or of the directing hand.

Springhall knew the directing hand. His mistake was to engage himself in espionage when the British Communist Party had completely swung to support of the war after Hitler's attack on Russia. He was detected passing on to Soviet intelligence secret information supplied by adherents within the Air Ministry, particularly the Marxist sympathiser, Captain Ormond Uren, who was also sentenced to seven years' penal servitude. Although Springhall was a dedicated Communist, Moscow ordered him to be sacrificed in order to preserve good relations and to promote the open exchange of scientific information with its new ally Great Britain. Harry Pollitt expelled Springhall from the Central Committee of the Party and denied any knowledge of his spying activities. In the House of Commons, the Home Secretary, Herbert Morrison, was asked whether he was suggesting that the Communist Party was officially responsible for acts of espionage. 'The facts speak for themselves,' the Home Secretary replied, 'and everybody can draw his own conclusions.'

Springhall's spying was an extreme folly. When so many Marxist scientists were employed in British defence work and might be ready to pass on scientific information to their new ally Russia without need of espionage, a leading Communist Party official caught in a primitive piece of spying was an embarrassment. He had to be disowned. As Brecht wrote in *The Threepenny Opera*, 'What was robbing a bank compared with owning a bank?' And what was spying for scientific information compared with collecting it openly from sympathizers?

7 Security Risk

'The world stopped for us in 1933,' Sid Quinn declared of his comrades from the International Brigades in Spain. Even though they tried to fight Fascism in the Second World War, it was not the same. As Communists, they were not acceptable in many regiments in the British army. They were feared politically as people who might indoctrinate the ranks and advocate mutinies. Some became Bevin Boys in the coal mines; others joined the Home Guard; others helped radical scientists such as Haldane in their experiments. Even the ending of the Nazi–Soviet Pact with Hitler's attack on Russia, did not end their quarantine. Although Russia was now one of the Allies, Communists were still distrusted by the military in Britain. They may now have been able to serve, as Cyril Connolly noted in his book on Burgess and Maclean, their own and their adopted country without a conflict. They were double patriots. Waverers might return to their allegiance and those who had never wavered be suddenly respected. But few in power thought that the alliance with Russia was more than an expedient to defeat Hitler. Who knew whether the Allied armies might not eventually confront the Red Army over the ruins of the Third Reich in a third world war?

This quarantine was not inflicted on leading scientists from the left wing. They were essential to the war effort and knew they were. They stayed close to each other throughout the war, particularly in the dining club called the Tots and Quots because Desmond Bernal had inscribed a copy of his neo-Marxist analysis of society, *The Social Function of Science* to Zuckerman: 'To Solly, *Quot Homines, Tot Sententiae*, D.': it was a favourite Latin tag of Jack Haldane's.

Marxism was much discussed in the club, but in Zuckerman's opinion, only two were Marxists, while the other members were mostly 'left of centre' and politically naïve. At a meeting of the club in 1940, Cockcroft was introduced as a member by J.G.Crowther and found himself sitting with Bernal, Zuckerman, Haldane, Blackett, Hyman Levy and the philanthropic Lord Melchett: they were to listen to Roy Harrod reading a paper on post-war Socialist economic policy, and to F.A.Lindemann reminding them that the war had first to be won before they could consider the future of science. The object of the meeting was to persuade the publisher Allen Lane to issue a paperback, *Science in War*, attacking the government for not mobilizing enough scientists to help in the fight against Fascism. While putting the finishing touches to the book, Zuckerman and Bernal were interrupted by the arrival in London of two of the directors of the French National Scientific Research Council, who had with them the only supply outside Norway of 'heavy water', that necessary aid to nuclear fusion.

After the Germans had attacked the Russians and broken their non-aggression pact, the chief guest at the Tots and Quots was Maysky, the Soviet ambassador in London. Anglo-Soviet scientific co-operation was the subject of discussion: it should be as open as Anglo-American co-operation. Blackett pointed out that the Russians needed fighter squadrons and a second front more than scientific exchanges, otherwise Russia might soon collapse. Maysky declared that he had absolute faith in the ultimate victory of his country, but he did not know the great price which his country would have to pay. Nor did he know what price the western Allies would have to pay for Russian victory. But the greater the co-operation, particularly in science, the lower the price would be for all. It was Maysky whom Burgess later accused Churchill himself of providing with information about what the government was thinking, when he was in opposition. Burgess claimed to Stephen Spender that he and Donald Maclean were in much the same position as Churchill. He said to Spender that, 'during the war, there were frequent exchanges of information between the British and the Russians, in which the rules of secrecy were more or less ignored, or considered to be suspended.'

Although the government was not actually convinced that it should exchange information with the Russians, it recognized the necessity for scientific advisers, especially drawn from the members of the Tots and Quots. Experts from this other 'culture' were more essential than intelligence operators drawn from the arts. Radical and Communist scientists played larger and larger roles in the war effort as their use and brilliance were proved. Blackett became director of Operational Research at the Admiralty, calculating the optimum size for convoys, including those sailing to Russia after 1942 to deliver war material. Bernal was finally employed as a scientific adviser by Combined Operations under Lord Louis Mountbatten, who did not care about anybody's politics as long as they were professional, unorthodox and effective. Bernal worked closely with Solly Zuckerman on many projects. Julian Huxley found it a strange chance that the two chief scientific advisers to the War Cabinet on the effects of bombing should be an expert in biochemistry and a specialist in the sexual behaviour of baboons. In fact, monkeys were used in the first tests to calculate the effects of bomb blasts on human beings.

Bernal had emphasized in *The Social Function* that science and war had always been connected; the novelty was not to recognize the connection. Under the stimulus of war, the rate of application of many scientific discoveries was far greater than in peacetime. With Zuckerman, he worked on the operational analysis of the devices, techniques and equipment needed for landing in Europe. They were the boffins for D-Day. They were joined by another radical but amateur scientist, Geoffrey Pyke, considered a poor security risk by the Americans. Together they were known as Mountbatten's Department of Wild Talents. Bernal particularly worked on the physics of beach formation and gave an effective demonstration to the Chiefs of Staff on the merits of artificial harbours by sinking paper ships in a bath stirred up by a junior officer making waves with a scrubbing brush.

When Mountbatten was asked about Bernal's commitment to the defeat of Nazism as part of his commitment to the aid of the Soviet Union, he merely stressed Bernal's generosity of action and mind. Even Zuckerman, soon to be sent to the Mediterranean theatre of war, admitted that his friend Bernal almost always knew both sides to a quesion. 'He had not been brought up by Jesuits for nothing.' So it was that Bernal remained a security risk, and most of the leading civilian advisers and war scientists found themselves excluded from the War Room as D-Day approached. They were not informed of the date or even the precise plan for the landing in Europe. Military secrecy now dictated all.

Political considerations as well as military ones had profound repercussions on the employment of scientists as well as on strategic policy. Once Winston Churchill became Prime Minister, his close friend and adviser F.A.Lindemann displaced Tizard as the chief influence on the Committee of Air Defence. He was responsible for supporting the Air Ministry in the misguided decision to try saturation bombing of cities in Germany, in spite of some opposition from Tizard and Blackett. The policy caused huge casualties among British and American air crews and among German civilians; it hardly impeded Nazi war production. Albert Speer could reassure Hitler, worried that the Allies might bomb German synthetic oil plants, that the enemy also had an Air Staff, bound to make the wrong decisions. It did, aided by some of its scientific advisers. Blackett also happened to be the only member of the MAUD committee to oppose the manufacture of the atomic bomb. He was outvoted, and the Manhattan Project went ahead with full British co-operation.

Churchill had stimulated atomic research in 1941 by forming a directing body under the name of Tube Alloys and the leadership of Sir Wallace Aken of Imperial Chemical Industries. At a later meeting with Franklin Roosevelt, Churchill informed the American President of the advances made in nuclear research in England and agreed to support a massive programme to manufacture atomic weapons before the end of the present war.

> We both felt painfully the dangers of doing nothing. We knew what efforts the Germans were making to procure supplies of 'heavy water' – a sinister term, eerie, unnatural, which began to creep into our secret papers. What if the enemy should get the atomic bomb before we did!

Although French scientists had brought to England all the 'heavy water' then available, Churchill sent in saboteurs to Norway to destroy the 'heavy water' plant there, while Roosevelt established the Manhattan Project under the extraordinary J.Robert Oppenheimer. Important atomic research work was still carried out at laboratories at Columbia University in New York and at the University of Chicago as well as at Berkeley with its huge cyclotron, but an atomic city was established at Los Alamos in New Mexico to co-ordinate all. By the last year of the war, some two hundred thousand scientists, engineers and research assistants were working at producing the first atomic bomb at a cost of two billion dollars. Only the United States had the intellect, reserves and commitment to develop the weapon so quickly.

To most scientists, the project was no misuse of the best minds in creating a devastating weapon. At Los Alamos, the Englishman James Tuck found 'a spirit of Athens, of Plato, of an ideal republic', where J.Robert Oppenheimer directed the most exclusive club in the world. Oppenheimer himself called the group of scientists working on the atomic bomb, 'a remarkable community, inspired by a high sense of mission, of duty and of destiny, coherent, dedicated, and remarkably selfless ... devoted to a common purpose.' That common purpose proved the philosophy of such scientific advisers to governments as Solly Zuckerman, who believed that a state of war could stimulate the scientist to great feats of the imagination. In a world of conflicting powers, science was both the arsenal and the instrument of power, but it was always a neutral arsenal and instrument. 'We cannot invest pure scientific knowledge with any inherent moral distinction. That is imparted by the way science is used.' Such an excuse salved the conscience of those scientists making the weapons of mass destruction for the politicians to choose to use.

Paradoxically, the creators of the atomic bomb for the Allies were often refugees from the Axis powers. One of them was Bruno Pontecorvo, a specialist in the design of 'heavy water' reactors. He had fled from Fascist Italy to France because he was Jewish and had relatives in high positions in his home Communist Party. He worked with the Communist French physicist, Joliot-Curie, before fleeing on to the United States in 1940. Three years later he was asked to join the British nuclear research project at Chalk River along with another Communist scientist, Allan Nunn May. Neither man was properly cleared by the British security service. Both were to pass atomic secrets to the Soviet government.

Another Italian physicist, Enrico Fermi, made some of the more valuable contributions to the discovery of the atomic bomb. He had fled from Rome for fear of persecution of his Jewish wife. Other émigré physicists such as Peierls and Fuchs moved on from England to Los Alamos. Niels Bohr was smuggled via Sweden and England to the United States, where he openly expressed his wish that some of the secrets of the fission bomb should be shared with the Soviet Union in order to defuse any post-war conflicts and rivalries. Churchill himself interviewed Bohr and dismissed any possibility of the international control of the atomic bomb. Roosevelt was more sympathetic to Bohr's approach, but was dissuaded by Churchill from sharing atomic knowledge with Stalin's government. Churchill even advocated Bohr's arrest for his support of disclosing nuclear discoveries to the Russians. In C.P.Snow's opinion, the British Prime Minister had a naïve faith in keeping secrets. Even though he was told by leading authorities that the Soviets would soon make an atomic bomb themselves, he deluded himself into not believing it. He felt that the possession of the bomb would give Britain and America a temporary dominion for at least a decade. It was to be more temporary and hardly worth the damage to international understanding.

Curiously enough, in Germany itself, where Hahn had completed nuclear fission of the uranium atom in 1938, the research group under Heisenberg had made little progress in perfecting a bomb before the defeat of Germany. Hitler allocated too few resources to making an atomic weapon, too many to developing rockets with inadequate warheads. Nazi progress on nuclear fission had been overestimated through fear, just as Soviet progress had been underestimated through hope and contempt. On 6 July 1945, the sun was judged to rise twice in a 'false dawn' in the desert of New Mexico. It was the test explosion of the first American atomic bomb under the unfortunate code-name of Trinity. The head of the Manhattan Project, J.Robert Oppenheimer, did not intend the name to refer to the Christian Trinity, but rather to the Hindu one of Brahma and Shiva and Vishnu, the Creator and the Destroyer and the Preserver of the peace. 'Now we're all sons of bitches', the director of the atomic test told Oppenheimer, while one of the observing generals merely stated: 'The war's over.' The great physicist Isador Rabi felt that an ancient equilibrium in nature had been upset. Human beings were now a threat to the world given them to live in.

On 6 August an atomic weapon using uranium 235 was dropped on the Japanese city of Hiroshima; three days later, a plutonium bomb was dropped on Nagasaki. The war against Japan, indeed, was over. Oppenheimer later declared that the scientists had learned sin. They had learned more. They had learned their own power. To Oppenheimer's credit, he joined three other leading physicists, Enrico Fermi and Ernest Lawrence and A.H.Compton, in writing to the Secretary of War that, although the development of more atomic weapons was a natural element in maintaining American military strength, they had grave doubts if such a development could contribute essentially or permanently to the prevention of war. 'We believe that the safety of this nation – as opposed to its ability to inflict damage on an enemy power – cannot be wholly or even primarily in its scientific or technical prowess. It can be based only on making future wars impossible.' Leonard Cheshire, the British observer of the dropping of the bomb on Nagasaki, came to the same conclusion. There was something so final about the sight of the explosion, a fireball suspended on a column 60,000 feet high, that this must mean not only the end of the Second World War, but of all war.

Allied scientific and technical prowess had finally made the atomic bomb possible. If a sin of politicians is an ignorance of the effects of their major decisions, a sin of scientists and sorcerer's apprentices is the urge to experiment at all costs to see what happens. No proof without tests, even at the expense of children's lives, both with bombs and chemicals. Solly Zuckerman might use his monkeys to study the effects of bomb blasts on *Homo sapiens*, but the atomic scientists allowed the badly-briefed American President and British Prime Minister to allow the study of the results of atomic explosions on human beings, not once, but twice. It was a way to end a war in the Far East, but it was also a gigantic laboratory test on what radiation might do to living beings and to the unborn.

Although the nuclear scientists would not accept responsibility for the dropping of the atom bombs on Japanese civilians, they had not warned the politicians who chose to drop the weapons of the consequences of using them. The initiators of the Manhattan Project, Franklin Roosevelt and Winston Churchill, had been succeeded by Harry Truman and Clement Attlee, who later declared that neither of them had known atomic weapons were different from high-explosive bombs, except in their greater force. Nothing was said about the genetic effects of a nuclear explosion or of fall-out. Attlee did not find out whether the scientists concerned knew or guessed of these terrible consequences. But if they did, they said nothing to those who had to make the final decision.

Before the successful explosion of atomic bombs by the Americans, Churchill had decided that Britain must manufacture its own nuclear devices. Cockcroft had been ordered to Canada to become the overlord of research into atomic fission there. With him had gone a youngish Cambridge physicist, Dr Allan Nunn May. After the defection of a Russian cypher clerk Igor Guzenko in September 1945, a Soviet spy ring was discovered in Canada, and Nunn May was proved to have accepted $700 and two bottles of whiskey, and to have given a sample of uranium 235 to a Soviet intelligence officer. Nunn May was known to be a Marxist and a radical member of the Cambridge branch of the Union of Scientific Workers, but such affiliations had been no hindrance in his contribution to atomic projects at a time when Russia was Britain's ally. The espionage actually took place before any overt estrangement between the British and Soviet governments. Given the small sums of money involved, Nunn May appeared to have acted for ideological reasons, not for real gain. He claimed that he had a higher right than loyalty to his country: he had the right of a private citizen to make a contribution 'to the safety of mankind'. The British judge who sentenced him to ten years' penal servitude declared that he had acted with degradation. Tom Driberg's estimation of him and other atomic scientists convicted of treason was more just. However wrong their actions might have been, they were inspired by a genuine opposition to the incurable evils of western society and to American policy in the Far East. It was, as the Labour cabinet minister Richard Crossman once said, an age of treason. And in such an age – as in the religious wars of the sixteenth and seventeenth centuries – conscientious traitors might be found on both sides. Conscientious objectors, however, were only found on one side.

In fact, Allan Nunn May had not contributed to the safety of mankind. He had made a very small contribution to power politics and the post-war settlement of Europe. He had provided Soviet agents with some necessary uranium samples. The Russians had openly approached the Americans for sixteen tons of uranium oxide and nitrate, but they had been fobbed off with export licences for a mere fourteen hundred and fifty pounds and a thousand grams of 'heavy water'. Churchill wanted all knowledge of the atomic bomb kept from Stalin, but the Americans felt that the Soviet dictator should be told at the Potsdam Conference. When he was told, Stalin showed no surprise. He knew already from his intelligence services. He crudely said that the question of the Balkan states and the governments of eastern Europe after the end of the war would be settled by power. This made Churchill demand the dropping of the first atomic bomb on Japan as soon as it might be ready so that Stalin might see 'where power really lay'. Only Churchill himself had lost power in England when the decision to drop the first bombs was taken.

The exclusive possession of usable nuclear weapons only gave the West a brief period of power, and espionage hardly affected its duration. The atomic secrets passed to the Russians by Nunn May and other émigré scientists working on the Atomic Research Project, such as Klaus Fuchs and Bruno Pontecorvo, may have accelerated the Soviet acquisition of a workable atomic bomb by a year or two. Their contribution, however, was a jot and a tittle compared to the common knowledge of theoretical physics shared between the United States, England, France and Russia. The euphoria of secrets, C.P.Snow pointed out in *Science and Government*, was usually combined with the euphoria of gadgets. Scientists such as Lindemann, who suffered from both euphorias should be kept from the decision-making processes of government, if right choices were to be made. In point of fact, societies at the same level of technology produced similar inventions. It would be odd if the United States of America or Russia kept for a long time a lead in military technology from one another. It was unrealistic and very dangerous to believe that the western powers would always be superior in military inventions to the eastern bloc. History and science did not work that way, and obsessive secrecy was no way to stop a rival power from developing similar weapons systems. As Snow testified on behalf of British scientists:

> The news of the first atomic pile reached a few of us in England in 1943. In the somewhat inelegant language of the day, we knew the atomic bomb was on. We heard people, intoxicated by the discovery, predicting that it would give the United States unheard-of power for so long as one could foresee. We did not believe it. We had no special prescience, but we were outside the area of euphoria. We speculated on how long it would take a country with the scientific and technical capacity of Russia to catch up, once the discovery was known. We guessed about six years. We were wrong. One always overestimates these periods. It took them four.

The Allied contribution to the Soviet cause in wartime was rarely scientific and hardly political. It was military, through the supply of war material and direct attack on the Axis powers. Hard pressed by the German armies in a long campaign of retreat that was to leave twenty million Russians dead, Stalin was desperate for the Allies to begin a second front in Europe to force Hitler to withdraw his divisions from the eastern sector as a counter to the new threat. The delay in opening that second front in France until after the German defeat at Stalingrad seemed to the Soviets to prove that the Allies wished Russia to be defeated or reduced to military impotence, unable to play a major role in any post-war settlement. Klaus Fuchs, who had been recruited by Peierls to work on the atomic bomb and was passing on nuclear secrets to the Soviet authorities, later gave as the reason for his treachery his complete confidence in Russian policy and belief that the Allies were deliberately allowing Germany and Russia to fight to the death. Stalin himself refused to declare war on Japan. He would not open a second front in the Pacific. There the western Allies could fight their own war of attrition in a murderous tit for tat.

The German advance into Russia had hurt the Soviet atomic programme. The important laboratories in Leningrad were evacuated in part. The physics institute in Moscow was unable to function for eighteen months. Another important research laboratory in Kharkov was seized by the Germans, although much of its equipment was secreted beyond the Ural Mountains. Raw materials were difficult to obtain, and transport to the uranium mines in Central Asia was impossible, after the German armies reached the Black Sea. Although Stalin urged Kapitsa and the other Russian physicists to press on with manufacturing an atomic weapon to use against the Germans, they were deprived of the goods and facilities they needed. At Los Alamos, there were no such problems. The United States was first able to solve the problem of the atomic bomb, the *Soviet Encyclopaedia* was to assert in 1950, because the Soviet Union bore the brunt of the war against Fascist Germany. And the Allies were not true allies in refusing to share atomic secrets in the common fight against the Nazi aggressor.

For the Communist Party of Great Britain the imperialists' war had become a struggle for the survival of the masses. The Party recruited new and old members, and regained influence in the factories. Although Douglas Springhall was expelled for being caught in the act of espionage, the party faithful were not discouraged from supplying information to Russia. As Douglas Hyde, then an editor of the *Daily Worker*, recalled:

The spying which had gone on during the 'Imperialist' war was nothing to that which followed. The information came from factories and the Forces, from civil servants and scientists. And the significant thing to recognise is that those who did it were not professional spies, they took big risks in most cases, received no payment whatsoever, and, this is doubly important, did not see themselves as spies, and still less as traitors.

Just as the abandoned war wives put many prostitutes out of business, so the plethora of ordinary Communists giving information to their war ally made trained Soviet agents almost superfluous during the last years of the war. Guy Burgess was a partial exception to the rule. Although he was no longer in the intelligence services, his broadcasting contacts and the coterie at Bentinck Street, where the Soviet agent and Czech diplomat Otto Katz was a regular visitor, made him able to fill courier bags to Moscow with political information. Through Desmond Bernal and possibly Goronwy Rees, he might learn of planning for D-Day, the Allied invasion of France, although not of its date, so urgently needed by Stalin. From Guy Liddell of MI5, he might hear the names of those in British intelligence. When interrogated about his relations with Burgess and Blunt after their treason was revealed, Victor (now Lord) Rothschild, felt it essential to disclose all he knew. He even had to suffer the false accusation that he was the 'fifth man' of the Cambridge spy ring, the scientist among them. He blamed himself for not realizing that some of the others were spies, but then, the nature of their calling hid their treachery from their closest friends. He remained sure that Guy Liddell, a brilliant and sensitive and delightful man, remained true to his country. Yet the revelations about Blunt destroyed Rothschild's confidence about all his Cambridge and Apostolic friends. 'For whom could I put my hand in the fire? I can still name a few and among them would, undoubtedly, be Guy Liddell.'

Atomic secrets were not passing through Bentinck Street to the Soviets, but directly from Klaus Fuchs. It was only in 1942 that Kim Philby learned of British research on nuclear fission through the dummy company called Tube Alloys. Investigating it led Philby to the Manhattan Project, then to the encouragement of Donald Maclean to accept the post of First Secretary at the British embassy at Washington, where he would have access to documents dealing with Anglo-American atomic research and could act as a contact between the Soviet scientific espionage rings already in place in the United States and in London.

Equally, the code-breaking secrets of German battle plans emanating from Bletchley Park were not passing through Bentinck

Street. Cambridge had fed its most brilliant talents into the crypto-graphers, who were unravelling the Nazi Enigma-machine codes by the processes called 'Ultra'. Among these talents was John Cairn-cross, who was instructed by his Soviet control to leave the Treasury and use his fluency in the German language to gain a post in Bletch-ley Park. He became an editor there in 1942, dealing with air intelli-gence. He supplied the Soviet embassy with classified documents, including Luftwaffe dispositions on the Russian front, which enabled the Soviet air force to destroy hundreds of enemy aeroplanes on the ground. In his later confessions to British intelligence, Cairn-cross claimed that the information supplied was to a wartime ally, even though its use by Russian forces might have warned the Ger-mans that their Enigma code was broken. Yet, as with the other Cambridge traitors, Cairncross's justification of this treason was specious. He had supplied his Soviet control with classified Treasury documents showing Britain's economic weakness during the Stalin–Hitler Pact, when Fascism and Bolshevism had been diplomatic bedfellows.

Kim Philby and Guy Burgess had little to do with passing on 'Ultra' decoded messages: even MI5 and MI6 were rationed with information in the interests of military security. Yet they knew of its paramount importance to the Russians, engaged in their death struggle with the Germans. Malcolm Muggeridge was present at a curious dinner at the Rothschild mansion in the Avenue Marigny after the liberation of Paris in 1944. Victor Rothschild had lent the house to British intelligence operations and was at the table there along with Kim Philby and Muggeridge. He vehemently opposed Churchill's decision to withhold from Stalin the Bletchley information about German battle plans on the eastern front; he did not know that Cairncross was supplying some of that informa-tion through the Lucy ring in Switzerland, where Alexander Foote was the radio operator. Rothschild seemed to Muggeridge to have lost his way, floundering somewhere between the Kremlin and the House of Lords, a Wise Man who had followed the wrong star to the wrong manger. But there was no question of his loyalty to his country or of his personal courage: he received the George Medal for defusing unexploded booby-traps.

In reply to him, Muggeridge argued that caution over the Bletchley material was legitimate, because the Russians had passed on to the Germans all they knew about the British during the Nazi–Soviet Pact. Another opportunity for treachery might occur. It was right to guard against it. Philby was outraged and stuttered that everything should be done to support the Red Army, even if the security of the Bletchley material was compromised. In Muggeridge's opinion, Philby would certainly have considered it proper and honourable to supply the Russians with the German decoded messages. In fact, Philby did not have access to them. He could only supply his Soviet colleagues with the names of British intelligence agents such as Muggeridge.

During the war, indeed, Burgess and the Bentinck Street coterie appear to have given little important information directly to the Soviet government. There was justice in Muggeridge's view of Burgess as an Etonian mudlark, the sick toast of a sick society. 'There was not so much a conspiracy gathered round him as just decay and dissolution. It was the end of a class, of a way of life; something that would be written about in history books.' Cyril Connolly agreed with this point of view, when he was to write on Burgess and Maclean after their defection. They were distinct from the atomic spies because they were members of the governing classes and high bureaucracy, not refugees like Fuchs and Pontecorvo, or obscure and humble figures like Nunn May. If traitors they were, then they were traitors to themselves, seeming to act against their own political interests.

The true role of Cambridge 'moles' during the war was still to burrow and rise. Burgess left the Talks Department of the BBC for the Press Department of the Foreign Office, then became the personal assistant of Hector McNeil, a journalist and Member of Parliament chosen by Ernest Bevin to be the Minister of State under him at the Foreign Office: Bevin had been picked by Clement Attlee to become Foreign Secretary for the Labour Party when Churchill and the Conservatives lost the general election of 1945. Ruffled at the promotion of an outsider, the Foreign Office assigned an official diplomat, Fred Warner, to serve alongside Burgess, who managed to become a friend of his enforced associate.

Philby's rise was even more spectacular. He drily noted that, as the Allies started to win the war, the Secret Intelligence Service began to think of the next enemy. Its thinking reverted to old and congenial channels, when its chief thrust had been the penetration of the Soviet Union and the defence of Britain against Bolshevism. Churchill himself had issued a minute in April 1944, that all secret establishments were being purged of Communists, 'because we know they owe no allegiance to us or to our cause and will always betray secrets to the Soviets, even while we are working together.' Philby was instructed by his Soviet control to do everything in his power to become head of section nine of the Secret Intelligence Service, which was in charge of counter-intelligence against Russia. Philby agreed to intrigue for the post and acquired it by acting ruthlessly against his superiors and inspiring trust in his own efficiency. The power even appeared to have been thrust upon him against his will. It was the case of a spy set to catch his own spy network. He was told not to communicate with American intelligence for fear that its agents might leak secrets to the Russians. For Philby, 'it was a piquant situation'. On one occasion, he even managed to arrange for Moscow to liquidate a prominent Soviet intelligence agent and would-be defector, Konstantin Volkov, before Volkov could betray him. With his cold wit Philby commented that the case was dead.

Philby's job as a Soviet officer was to prevent any effective intelligence being carried out against Russia, to inform the Russians about British intelligence agents and to pass on the little secret information that he had. It was surprising that his Communist affiliations in his youth and during his first marriage were not held against him. In fact, they inspired respect among his colleagues. He was thought to *know* about Communism and thus to be able to combat its influence. Even his wartime associates such as the historian Hugh Trevor-Roper admired him for his benign, distant irony. 'No one ever suggested he was in touch with any enemy. ... He was the blue-eyed boy of the establishment, the one "amateur" who was appreciated by the "professionals".' The fact that Philby's superiors suspended their suspicions in his case seemed to prove his indispensability. He had broken through the net and the political prejudices of the heads of security, who saw Communism as mere subversion, not a religion.

They underestimated its power to convert English gentlemen. They also believed that there was no way back for any convert. We thought that there were no Philbies; they insisted that all who had tasted communism were Philbies – except Philby himself. We believed that communist doctrine could not prevail over humanity. They believed that it could not prevail over class. We were all wrong.

Maclean had been posted to the British embassy in Washington, where he was appointed First Secretary and then the head of Chancery. He had access to all cyphers and codes. He could inform his Soviet control of American and British positions before the Yalta Conference, where the post-war influence of Russian power in eastern Europe was largely accepted. Later, Maclean was to be appointed joint secretary of the Combined Policy Committee on atomic energy, which made available to him the planning and secret data on the manufacture of nuclear weapons. Like Philby, Maclean was instructed by Russian intelligence agents to seek the position of their maximum advantage. Like Philby, he achieved it. Incredibly, there had been no security officer appointed in the Foreign Office before 1940, when Maclean had already been in the service for many years.

Blunt became personal assistant to the Security Service leader, Guy Liddell. Like Philby, he was able to provide his Soviet control with much information on security and counter-intelligence. The Apostle whom he had recruited at Cambridge, Leo Long, was working for MI14, a department that assessed German troop strengths and battle planning; it had access to the decoded German messages from Bletchley Park. Thus Long was able to supply Blunt with military information vital to the Russians even during the period of the Nazi–Soviet Pact, when such intelligence could have been passed back to the Germans, warning them to change their 'unbreakable' Enigma code. Long's revelations supplemented the material provided to the Kremlin by Cairncross. And when Blunt was assigned to SHAEF, Supreme Headquarters Allied Expeditionary Force, the planning organization for D-Day, he was also given access to the Bletchley decoded messages, providing a third source on German strategy for the Russians. Lieutenant-Colonel Noel Wild, the head of an operations and intelligence unit in SHAEF, suspected that the Russians fed back to German intelligence details of the Allied manoeuvres in France near the end of the war to enable Hitler to counterattack in the Ardennes and delay the advance of the democratic armies so that the unchallenged Red Army could swallow up all of eastern Europe. As Stalin said at Potsdam, power would decide the shape of the post-war Balkans. Communist countries developed behind the front line of the Soviet forces.

Yet scientific information was as important to the Kremlin as territorial advantage. The Red Army also competed with the western armies for the capture of leading German physicists and engineers, particularly those working in the fields of atomic and rocket research. More than two hundred German scientists, including the Nobel Prize winner, Dr Gustav Hertz, were brought back to Russia to work on nuclear projects. The Americans brought back the cream of the rocket engineers, who had invented the destructive V1s and V2s; among them was the later pioneer of lunar rockets, Werner von Braun, of whom it was said that he aimed at the moon, but sometimes hit London.

The Second World War was won by military power. If there was to be another world war, it would also be won by military power. Scientists had become the chief contributors to the weapons of war. While political espionage was useful, it was mainly of use if it served a military purpose. Of more use was the revelation of military secrets, particularly those affecting the greatest devices of mass destruction ever to be created, the uranium and hydrogen bombs. Arguably, Klaus Fuchs was the most valuable Soviet agent during and after the Second World War. Not only did he supply the Soviets with information on the essential early atomic research in England that resulted from the seminal paper produced by Frisch and Peierls in 1941, but he was invited to Los Alamos along with Peierls and other émigré physicists to work on the Manhattan Project.

He was popular there, Edward Teller remembered, because he was kind and helpful and interested in what everybody else was doing. He was also as close-mouthed as a good spy should be. Mrs Peierls called him 'Penny-in-the-Slot' Fuchs, because a sentence had to be dropped into him before he would produce a sentence in return. His cover was the opposite of the garrulous Burgess or even of Alexander Foote, who used to boast to his Swiss friends that he was a spy, only to provoke laughter and disbelief because he looked like a Yorkshire insurance agent.

Fuchs supplied his atomic information to the Soviet authorities through Harry Gold, a reliable Russian agent. When he was discovered, Gold identified another atomic spy at Los Alamos, David Greenglass, who in turn denounced Julius and Ethel Rosenberg. Other Soviet agents acquired information about the radiation laboratory at Berkeley through Steve Mesarosh, also called Steve Nelson, a member of the National Committee of the American Communist Party, who used a Communist research physicist Joseph Weinberg to reveal the secrets of the cyclotron and other atomic discoveries. Through the Marxist professor Haakon Chevalier, Nelson even approached J.Robert Oppenheimer for information before he became the head of the Manhattan Project, but Oppenheimer denounced them to the American security forces. In Chicago, an old Bolshevik, Arthur Adams, searched out data on the atomic plant at Oak Ridge and on uranium stockpiles in the United States; he was aided by the chemist Clarence Hiskey, another member of the American Communist National Committee, who worked on plutonium at Columbia University and in the metallurgical laboratory at Chicago. Through these sources, the Russian physicists acquired knowledge of the latest developments and processes in atomic research abroad. What the Allies would not supply openly to aid the Soviet war effort was gathered by secret agents. Espionage meant the pursuit of scientific intelligence by other means.

At the trial of the Rosenbergs for spying in 1951, the judge condemned their actions in the strongest terms. 'In murder,' he declared, 'a criminal kills only his victim.' But the Rosenbergs had put into Russian hands the secret of the atomic bomb years before American scientists had predicted the Russians would acquire a usable one. The result, the judge pronounced, was the Communist aggression in Korea with the loss of fifty thousand American lives as well as the threat of a nuclear holocaust in America itself. The judge did not believe in nuclear parity or in a balance of deterrence as a way of keeping the peace and of preventing a third world war. He believed that the United States would never use atomic weapons against Russia, although it had used them against Japanese civilians at Hiroshima and Nagasaki. The atomic spies, however, believed that they were aiding the safety of mankind by passing on the secrets of the atomic bomb to Russia, which would never use the weapon except in its own self-defence. Russia was also a war ally, and Communist scientists maintained that they should give all research knowledge to Moscow, especially if it were of military use in the fight against Fascism.

When Klaus Fuchs was put on trial, he was not tried for high treason, which incurred the death penalty, because his spying began in 1942 after Russia had become Britain's ally: high treason meant directly aiding an enemy. Yet those who had supplied the Russians with classified intelligence during the Nazi–Soviet Pact were guilty of indirectly aiding an enemy, and these were the Cambridge spies, less important and more arrogant in their treachery and foreign allegiance. Not for them the controlled schizophrenia of a Fuchs, who confessed that his mental processes were affected by his devotion to Communism, so that the dominant half of his mind led him to do things which the other half recognized quite clearly were wrong. When he had left the company of other Marxists to work at Harwell among a great many English scientists without strong radical convictions, but with a deep-rooted firmness that enabled them to live a decent way of life, Fuchs's own convictions had been shaken until he was ready to reveal his treachery. Conscience does not always make cowards of us all. Moral cowardice made Fuchs continue for many years to do what he knew was wrong, until finally it provoked his conscience to confess and be judged.

8 Conscientious Fission

'This has killed a beautiful subject,' the leading Australian physicist Mark Oliphant said, after the bombing of Hiroshima and Nagasaki. He had been a pupil of Rutherford, he had supported the open exchange of scientific knowledge. He now knew that theoretical physics would be constrained by secrecy, contorted by military application, and convulsed by moral doubts among the physicists. Desmond Bernal, who was still working at the centre of the military machine when the bombs were dropped, considered the officers in uniform surrounding him as out of date as the Yeomen of the Guard. A Chief of Staff had said to him, 'At the beginning of the war, strategy dictated weapons, but at its end it was weapons that dictated strategy.' That was now true. Bernal looked at the misuse of atomic fission as a gross betrayal of science, which was no longer an automatic force in human progress, but also a factor in human regress.

C. P. Snow did not share Bernal's point of view, nor did the physicists working on the atomic bombs. Most scientists believed that Nazism was near absolute evil. Since the Nazis might make their own nuclear weapons, then the Allies had to make theirs. The fact that the Nazis were defeated before any atomic bomb was made, and that the first two nuclear devices were used against the Japanese, did not destroy the purpose of making them. This was 'The Moral Un-Neutrality of Science' in Snow's opinion:

But the trouble is, when you get on to any kind of moral escalator, to know whether you're ever going to be able to get off. When scientists became soldiers they gave up something, so impercepti-

bly that they didn't realize it, of the full scientific life. Not intellec-
tually. I see no evidence that scientific work on weapons of maximum destruction has been in any intellectual respect different
from other scientific work. But there is a moral difference. It
may be... that this is a moral price which, in certain circum-
stances, has to be paid. Nevertheless, it is no good pretending
that there is not a moral price. Soldiers have to obey. That is
the foundation of their morality. It is not the foundation of the
scientific morality. Scientists have to question and if necessary
to rebel.

Snow was not stating that loyalty was without virtue or that all
rebellion was good. He was pointing out that loyalty could become
conformity, and that obedience carried to the limit could become
destructive. More crimes, as Nazi officialdom proved, could be carried out in the name of obedience than ever were in the name of
rebellion. Snow himself had become a government official rather
than a wartime scientist, and had fallen into the moral trap of
conformity. He was liable to hide behind an institution and refuse
moral choice.

That was not the attitude of radical scientists like Bernal and
Haldane. 'I believe that a scientist is all the more use in the world,'
Haldane wrote of his period as an active Communist writing for
the *Daily Worker*, 'if, like Benjamin Franklin, he takes an active
part in politics and does not always behave like a perfect gentleman.'
What had been regarded as legitimate political activity was now
regarded as sedition, both during and after the war. The thing
was to improve links with Russia, not to end them. In this spirit,
Desmond Bernal went to Moscow in June 1945, to attend a celeb-
ration of the 220th anniversary of the Academy of Sciences. He
began discussions on the foundation of an international body of
scientists to include Russian ones. This effort culminated in the
formation of the World Federation of Scientific Workers with
J.G.Crowther as its Secretary-General. Bernal was also interested
in the creation of Unesco which chose Julian Huxley as its first
Executive Secretary. Radicals persisted in believing that the open
exchange of scientific and technological information could survive

the winning of the war and the dissensions of the Allied powers.

Ideology, however, could harm the practice of science itself. The most notorious case involved Haldane and led to his leaving the Communist Party. The eminent Soviet geneticist N.I.Vavilov had been condemned as a British agent who subverted the theories of Stalin's protégé Lysenko; he had died in exile in Siberia during the war. At a meeting of the Soviet Academy of Sciences in 1948, twelve resolutions were passed: these damned Vavilov's genetics as unpatriotic because they were based on inherited characteristics; Lysenko's environmental genetics were holy writ, because they suited dialectical materialism and were blessed by the Soviet state.

> Science is no longer regarded in the U.S.S.R. [Julian Huxley remonstrated] as an international activity of free workers, whose prime interest it is to discover new truth and new facts, but as an activity subordinated to a particular ideology and designed only to secure practical results in the interests of a particular national and political system.

To Huxley, Marxism-Leninism had become a dogmatic religion and had turned from reform to persecution. He wickedly compared Lysenko's genetic dogmas to the fact that the Jews had circumcised their male children for five thousand years without affecting the shape of their inherited foreskins. 'There's a divinity that shapes our ends,' Huxley observed along with Hamlet, 'rough-hew them how we will.'

Haldane alone supported Lysenko's theories, although they were based on unsupported assertions. As Lysenko was discredited, so Haldane distanced himself from the supreme Russian geneticist. Other radical scientists found themselves losing their influence because of political changes and the beginning of the Cold War between Russia and the western Allies. With the Labour government coming to power in Britain, Lindemann fell from grace, as he had been Churchill's scientific adviser, and Tizard was recalled by the new Prime Minister Clement Attlee as chairman of the Advisory Council on Scientific Policy. Although Socialist in theory, the government suspected those with radical views, and Blackett found himself shunted to one side. He wrote three books attacking the

British government's decision to proceed with the manufacture of an atomic, and later a hydrogen bomb. He accused the United States of dropping its two nuclear bombs on Japan only to forestall the Russian occupation of Manchuria. He believed that the United States seriously considered a preventive war against the Soviet Union before 1953, when the first Russian hydrogen bomb was tested.

These nuclear weapons were also sought by successive British and French governments, determined not to be excluded from the great game of power play. The post-war Labour government recalled Cockcroft from Canada and put him in charge of the nuclear research establishment to be constructed at Harwell. In spite of British scientific collaboration with the Americans during the war, nothing much could be expected in return, what with the Nunn May spy case and the suspicion in Congress that there were Communist sympathizers among British scientists. Only real achievement on the part of the British nuclear physicists, Oliphant warned Cockcroft, could ensure full and willing collaboration with the Americans. As with radar, full exchange of secret information would only be had when American scientists felt it essential to visit England to keep in touch with advances in techniques and their application.

Efforts by leading scientists of all nations to secure the international control of atomic energy and to collaborate on research into its use for peace foundered in suspicion. The Macmahon Act, which prohibited the exchange of classified technical information with foreigners, including the British, passed Congress in August 1946. It was a signpost towards intermittent efforts by the United States to control the export of its scientific innovations, in order that it might retain its technological lead over all other countries. Like charity, invention should begin at home and stay there.

Only America's urgent need for uranium for its nuclear programme persuaded the government that some collaboration with the British nuclear research programme was possible. As usual, Cockcroft was the go-between. Britain gave up most of its supplies of uranium ore from the Belgian Congo in exchange for access to certain American discoveries on reactors and radioactivity. The production of plutonium in Britain, however, scared the Americans from their policy of closer collaboration, also the belief of some of the American Atomic Energy Commission led by Lewis Strauss that Britain was far to the left 'and therefore may give away the secrets to the Communists, some of whom already [sit] in Parliament'.

Yet efforts at the official level to obstruct the exchange of scientific information could not prevent Cockcroft personally from visiting his physicist friends at Los Alamos or from observing American advances in chemical separation, linear accelerators, cyclotrons and mass spectrography. Individually, leading scientists did aid each other. But official co-operation was set back by the Russian explosion of an atomic device in June 1947, while the Marshall Plan to save western Europe from Socialism through massive foreign aid was only three weeks old. Two years later in 1949, and two years before the British detonated their first nuclear weapon, the Russians set off two major nuclear explosions to remove rock barriers; the ignition systems of the first effective Soviet atomic weapons were based on material supplied by Klaus Fuchs. His conviction on charges of espionage, followed by the defections of Burgess and Maclean, further soured the possibility of scientific collaboration. Even Cockcroft failed to open the lines of communication across the Atlantic. As an American negotiator Carroll Wilson reported, the failure was 'due to the American distrust of any information going anywhere and the setbacks which Fuchs's and Maclean's defections and treachery gave to all of it'.

Espionage as usual had poisoned reciprocity. Treason was the enemy of reason. The escalation of the Cold War and the race to build the hydrogen bomb increased suspicions. The day after Fuchs confessed to passing atomic secrets on to the Russians, President Truman ordered work to proceed on the thermonuclear bomb designed by the conservative scientist Edward Teller. By opposing the development of this new weapon, J. Robert Oppenheimer found himself accused of being a security risk, denied access to classified information, and interrogated by a board appointed by the Atomic Energy Commission. In Russia, Kapitsa was also credited with refusing to collaborate in making hydrogen bombs. Along with developing processes for liquefying oxygen and creating microwave electronics, he had worked on aspects of creating the Russian atomic bomb in spite of direct denials to British scientists such as Solly Zuckerman on their visits to Moscow. In 1947, however, Kapitsa had used a former pupil of Abram Joffé, Professor P. L. Aleksandrov, the Soviet representative on the atomic energy commission of the United Nations, to appeal to friendly western scientists to stop research into nuclear weapons. This peace attempt was hated by Stalin. Communist Party members, more reliable than Kapitsa, although less brilliant as scientists, were put in charge of the fission programme. Bulganin, Malenkov and Beria from the Politburo led a special commission to control nuclear research. Without Kapitsa's co-operation, they were responsible for the swift development of effective atomic bombs during the next two years. The products of Soviet espionage were fed by Beria into the Russian nuclear weapons laboratories. In a real sense, European and North American Communist scientists aided in the manufacture of the first Russian atomic bombs, although these would have been made a year or two later without such secret intelligence.

With his knowledge of low-temperature research, Kapitsa was too important to be left out of the schedule to manufacture a hydrogen bomb. He was pardoned by Stalin and forced by Beria to leave his position as director of the Institute for Physical Problems in order to carry out secret work for the government. During the next decade before he returned to his official position, the Soviet Union developed a hydrogen bomb. Kapitsa appears to have refused to allow his institute to be used for work on thermonuclear explosions or to be controlled by the secret police or by the military; but he himself was prepared in principle to work on the hydrogen bomb. His reasons for baulking initially at the research were not the scruples of an Oppenheimer. In C. P. Snow's opinion, Kapitsa was a deep Russian patriot and would certainly have believed that his homeland should possess the hydrogen bomb if the Americans had it. He himself declared later to the Americans at a Pugwash conference seeking solutions to the nuclear arms race, 'Since your country had the bomb, my country would have to have it too.' He refused only to give over his institute to the misrule of the Soviet Ministry of Defence. He might have been defending the Cavendish from the misrule of Whitehall. The price was himself, a price he had paid before. 'He knew that on this kind of job he was as valuable as any man in the Soviet Union. He wanted his own way.' He got it. Ironically, he gave the young Andrey Sakharov the opportunity to further the production of the Russian hydrogen bomb, although Sakharov was to become one of the leading Soviet dissidents of the 1980s.

Whatever Kapitsa's reasons for trying to oppose the spread of nuclear weapons, he was an Oppenheimer in his own country, an organizer of funding and of research, a developer of 'big physics', and a supporter of the use of science in wartime. A reviewer of his essays in *Science* noted that both he and Oppenheimer rose by the help of the state, opposed their governments, fell from grace, and were rehabilitated as heroes. As statesmen of science, both expressed their concern for the survival of mankind in the nuclear age which they spawned.

After exploding an atomic bomb, it took the Americans four years to make a hydrogen bomb. It took the Russians four and a half years. The British and the French took a little longer. In Britain's case, the decision to produce the hydrogen bomb was seen by Churchill's Conservative cabinet as reducing the risk of war. It was feared that the United States might still intervene with nuclear weapons in Asia or make a pre-emptive attack on Russia. Britain's best chance of preventing this was to be the third nuclear power with thermonuclear weapons. 'In so far as any moral principle was involved,' a Cabinet minute read, 'it had already been breached by the decision of the Labour government to make the atomic bomb.'

So advances in weapons systems encouraged competitive governments to blame past decisions for present imperatives. Because one political party began a military programme, another party continued it. Because one power possessed an atomic bomb, another power felt obliged to acquire it. Britain and France refused to consider themselves lesser powers and proceeded to manufacture their independent nuclear weapons. Yet the Russians were far in advance of the British in spite of the contributions of scientists in England to the Manhattan Project. When the Russians exploded their effective nuclear bomb in 1949, Sir Henry Tizard, now the chief scientific adviser to the Ministry of Defence, gave pragmatic reasons for stopping the national nuclear programme. 'We are not a Great Power and never will be again,' he wrote. 'Let us take warning from the fate of the Great Powers of the past and not burst ourselves with pride (see Aesop's fable of the frog).'

His doubts were not heard by Labour or Conservative administrations. Britain pressed ahead with its nuclear programme. As the Cold War between the western democracies and the Communist powers intensified after the fall of China to Mao's armies, the pressure on scientists to aid their country's defence programme without moral queasiness grew greater. During the Second World War, Solly Zuckerman had been approached by an American general, who had said, 'When we've finished with Germany, we'll still want you when we take on the Russians. Don't forget.' Zuckerman never forgot the remark. It showed him that government scientific advisers would now and for ever be connected to the military machine. He was one of the scientists, indeed, who fought for the principle that they should not only evolve weapons and policies, but should be part of the analytic team, which drew conclusions from the use of the strategy, and which presented a final report. To leave judgement to some ignorant independent or civil servant belonged to the Wonderland that Alice knew. Scientists should provide the first intelligence to create policies and the last intelligence to evaluate their effect.

There had been an effort to destroy Germany's technology at the end of the war and to prohibit research there. Zuckerman knew that scientific knowledge could not be confined. He also distrusted military thinking without technical advice, and quoted Tacitus on many generals' wish for lasting devastation, 'When they make a wilderness, they call it peace.' Better an economic miracle in a reborn German republic than a permanent wasteland on the borders of Soviet-controlled eastern Europe. Science and technological change had become necessities in all countries and to all governments. The problem was; how could the scientists influence the governments and the military without serving them utterly? The question was no longer *quis custodiet ipsos custodes*, who will guard the guardians? It was *quantum scientiae sciant custodes*, how much science may the guardians know?

The protests of a few American, British and Russian scientists like Szilard and Seaborg, Blackett and Kapitsa, against the manufacture of nuclear weapons had no effect on their respective governments. The espionage of Klaus Fuchs aided the Russian manufacture of an atomic bomb just as the defection of Bruno Pontecorvo was to aid the making of a Russian hydrogen bomb. But their actions only accelerated inevitable discoveries by months or the odd year. The unique possession by the United States of atomic weapons for four years after 1945 did not prevent the fall of the world's largest population in China to Communist forces or the spread of Marxism across eastern Europe; ideology followed the Red Army, not the mushroom cloud. If the Russians had possessed the atomic bomb early in 1945, they would certainly have dropped it on Berlin, but hardly have used it thereafter. After using atomic bombs on Hiroshima and Nagasaki no American President authorized the dropping of the atomic or the hydrogen bomb, when the United States was their sole owner. Before there was a balance of nuclear deterrence between America and Russia, atomic weapons were rarely used as direct threats, blackmail or bargaining counters, except perhaps during the later Cuban missile crisis and the Vietnam War.

These were the political facts of the post-war years, when Russia and America, Britain and France were still officially allies. Arguably, it was the manufacture of nuclear weapons by Russia that led to the Cold War. The western nations no longer felt complacent because of their devastating explosive devices. Yet Russia's use of espionage to obtain secrets about these devices also led to a worsening of diplomatic relations, particularly as diplomats were suborned. The infiltration of Donald Maclean into the post of First Secretary at the British embassy at Washington gave him access to the Combined Policy Committee on Atomic Energy, where he sat with one other British representative, one Canadian, and three Americans, who might include the Secretary of Defense and David Lilienthal, the chairman of the American Atomic Energy Commission in charge of the nuclear programme. Maclean himself was a product of a Cambridge arts education; according to his friends, he did not know the difference between a hair-drier and a cyclotron. But aided by a British homosexual physicist, who was also a Marxist and a frequent visitor to Washington, Maclean could supply his Soviet contacts with full reports on the progress of American atomic research and the stockpiling of nuclear materials and weapons. He had access to all documents that passed through the Combined Policy Committee; he would copy them and hand them to Soviet agents. He was a regular visitor to the archives, laboratories and plants of the Atomic Energy Commission, and knew most of its top technicians. With Klaus Fuchs, he was even a delegate to a conference in Washington in November 1947, to decide on the declassification of wartime nuclear secrets. When Senator Hickenlooper declared in 1949 that there was Communist infiltration at the commission, it was no McCarthyite smear. Maclean was the mole in the atom.

In spite of, or paradoxically because of, Senator McCarthy's crusade against clandestine Communists within the American government, the British government continued to trust ex-Communists in its own ranks and services. Sexual deviance was still no bar to promotion, although it was an obvious opportunity for blackmail by Soviet intelligence agents. Flaws in personal behaviour were even treated as proof of independence of character, as if inside every scandalous civil servant a Lawrence of Arabia was bursting to get out. The novelist Anthony Powell knew both Maclean and Burgess in the post-war years. He found Maclean drunken and violent, unreliable and bisexual and inordinately conceited. Yet Maclean remained a typical civil servant by wanting to appear different. His behaviour paradoxically confirmed his conventional profession. Burgess, however, was generally known as a notorious scallywag, unfit to be trusted with the smallest responsibility or the least secret. Yet he was trusted with responsibilities and secrets by the Labour Member of Parliament, Hector McNeil, Minister of State for Foreign Affairs. Powell quoted Winston Churchill's alleged remark about Tom Driberg, also a Labour Member of Parliament and Burgess's friend, as if the remark were intended for Burgess: 'He has the unenviable reputation of being the only man in this House who has brought buggery into disrepute.'

Burgess would treat confidential papers like confetti on his Whitehall desk. A studied carelessness hid his secret intentions. Slovenliness disguised his treachery. He even persuaded his colleague Fred Warner that he had no interest in the papers inside the Minister's boxes, although Warner later admitted this might have been a bluff on his part. It was. The anti-Soviet policy taken by Clement Attlee and his Foreign Minister Ernest Bevin and his deputy McNeil was of great interest to the Kremlin. Burgess would often quote to Warner from his fellow Apostle, E.M.Forster, the misused line about betraying one's country rather than one's friend. Warner believed that Burgess meant it. Friendship mattered to him, his country did not.

Burgess still used the Apostles and the remnants of the Bloomsbury group to gather intelligence which he could deliver in his regular espionage reports to his Russian contacts. The bisexual Harold Nicolson, husband of Vita Sackville-West and a Conservative Member of Parliament, was one of Burgess's sources. His friend and biographer, James Lees-Milne, wrote that there was 'little doubt that Burgess extracted from Harold inside information which he passed on to his masters in Moscow'. Nicolson, like many other friends of Burgess, chose to ignore his unreliability and frequent revelations of Soviet preferences. The tie among homosexuals, the old school tie, and the unspoken rule among members of the ruling élite that they could not betray one another even for their country were enough to keep Nicolson's mouth sealed. Burgess was 'just soaked and silly' and made Nicolson angry. He agreed with Goronwy Rees that Burgess's increasing dependence on drugs as well as drink, his morose and flamboyant behaviour, made it impossible for him to be a Soviet agent.

The most efficient of these, Kim Philby, was only capable of minor betrayals in the post-war years. He may have sent thirty British intelligence agents abroad to their deaths, while he was running the Soviet Affairs section of the reconstructed Secret Service. He was transferred to the British embassy in Turkey as First Secretary. He had now denounced hundreds of Albanian exiles, who were being sent back to Albania to lead a counter-revolution. Philby was then recalled to London to serve as a representative of British intelligence in Washington, working with the Central Intelligence Agency and the Federal Bureau of Investigation. There he was followed by Guy Burgess, who had so much disgraced himself by his drunkenness and homosexuality, that inexplicably he was given a last chance to make good as a Second Secretary in the British embassy in the United States. At Burgess's farewell party in London, Goronwy Rees noticed Anthony Blunt, three senior members of the British security services, the homosexual Wolfgang zu Puttlitz, and Burgess's young male partner and general factotum, Jimmy. Hector McNeil advised Burgess not to mention three things to the Americans: Communism, homosexuality and the colour bar. Burgess promised not to make a pass at Paul Robeson.

Donald Maclean was, however, recalled from Washington and sent to the British embassy in Egypt, where he also ruined himself by continual drunkenness and acts of violence, including smashing up an apartment with Philip Toynbee, and breaking a colleague's leg in a brawl on the Nile. He was returned to London to undergo psychiatric treatment instead of a security investigation. He fell back into a life of booze, bars and boy-friends. He was tipsy and indiscreet enough to accuse Goronwy Rees in the Gargoyle Club: 'You used to be one of us, but you ratted.' He laughed as he told other diplomats he was 'working for Uncle Joe'. Incredibly, he was recalled to head the American department at the Foreign Office, as if alcoholic promiscuity was a passport to preferment. At his desk, he would and did copy for the Soviet Union all documents relevant to policies affecting the Russian government and to the Allied war in Korea. General MacArthur, indeed, used to complain that the Chinese seemed always to have intelligence about his order of battle. Although the American and British security services were becoming aware of Maclean's blatant espionage, the Foreign Office still seemed ready to protect its own.

The fourth member of the Cambridge traitors, Anthony Blunt, had an extraordinary translation. He succeeded Sir Kenneth Clark as Surveyor of the King's Pictures and became director of the Courtauld Institute, leaving his official post in intelligence. Before he left, however, he performed a mission that won him the gratitude of the Royal Family. Its German cousins through the marriage of Queen Victoria's eldest daughter, the Hesse family, had become advisers to Hitler, who exempted them from the Führer Edict banning members of the German aristocracy from holding important posts in the Third Reich because of blood ties with aristocrats abroad. Prince Philipp of Hesse married an Italian princess and acted as the link between Hitler and Mussolini, also as the intermediary between Hitler and the Duke and Duchess of Windsor, who visited Germany after the abdication crisis. At the Hesse castle near Frankfurt, there were compromising documents dealing with the Windsors' connection with prominent Nazi leaders, who wished ex-King Edward VIII to aid them in securing a treaty with England. Also at the castle were thousands of Queen Victoria's letters to her eldest daughter, briefly the Empress of Germany, many of them dealing with sensitive political matters in Anglo–German relations. The castle was occupied by corrupt American intelligence operatives, more interested in discovering where the Hesse jewels had been hidden than in unearthing documents that might embarrass the British Royal Family. Blunt successfully broke into the castle, retrieved the papers of Queen Victoria and the Duke of Windsor, and returned with them to the Royal Archives at Windsor Castle, where they were kept until the Nazi collaborators among the Hesse family were cleared by the Occupation authorities in Germany and restored to their possessions and estates.

The fifth Cambridge traitor and fellow Apostle, Leo Long, was seconded to the Control Commission for Germany. He was to become deputy head of British intelligence there. Blunt visited him and tried to recruit him as his replacement in MI5 in London, but Long was not selected. He continued to pass on intelligence to the Russians. Also serving at the Control Commission as the British representative in the political division after a wartime career in the Joint Intelligence Staff in the War Cabinet Office was Noel Annan, who was to become an Apostle and the Provost of King's College and a leading influence on the secret society. He devoted himself to learning German and the arts of government; he would become a peer and one of the great administrators of his generation, succeeding Sir Edward Marsh as an orchestrator of the right people in high places.

Annan is an observer, chronicler and moulder of generations. He noticed a significant change in Cambridge undergraduates by the beginning of the fifties. The amateurs of the arts of his age were being replaced by students who were interested in becoming professionals, particularly in communications. Even the homosexual cult began to disappear, although it was prevalent in King's College in the early years after the war. Raymond Leppard, who went up to Trinity to read music in 1948, put King's second only to his own college. The other place had a special aura 'and Kingsmen always gave the impression of having been, like the twelve, chosen – often, we thought, more for their looks than for intellectual or social talent.' Of course, many Kingsmen were chosen, like the twelve, also to become Apostles.

Within the college there was a delightfully titillating undercurrent of homosexuality, man-about-townery, café-society sophistication that we didn't necessarily want, but envied nevertheless. The high-table – now rendered sadly low – was full of people who remembered Rupert Brooke and knew the Bloomsbury group; Keynes, Lytton Strachey, the Woolfs, a world that has of late been so wearisomely oversung. There was enough glamour in it for returning service men to be dazzled, and, I suppose, it was good for us to have been dazzled.

But there was a new seriousness about. The university atmosphere was different after the Second World War. This had not been an unnecessary slaughter, the flower of a generation seemingly sacrificed by guilty old men. It appeared to have been the Last Just War there ever might be. Far fewer young men had lost their lives far more democratically in order to resist and destroy the bestiality of Fascism, which had murdered many millions of Jews and Slavs in its concentration camps. Although the post-war years under a Labour government were an age of rationing and austerity, they only seemed to prolong the necessary sacrifice. The Conservative governments of 1951 and thereafter were to herald an age of affluence. This suited a generation of war children, hardened by hostile conditions and deprivation to acquire a discipline and wish to work for a better life. There were now beavers by the Cam, where once there had been butterflies.

The immediate post-war generation of Oxford graduates was to be far more influential than the Cambridge one. In an effort to escape their educational privileges, some of its members became self-consciously classless and temporarily militant. Goaded by the abrasive wit of Kenneth Tynan, soon to become the most influential theatre critic of his time, directors and politicians and writers of future significance appeared to capture that intellectual rigour and moral commitment that had been associated with Cambridge. Anthony Wedgwood Benn began the tortuous political road that would lead him from the House of Lords to captain the radical wing of the Labour Party, while Peter Brook and Tony Richardson and Lindsay Anderson, the son of a major-general, would revolutionize the staging and content of plays and films to come. Even Kingsley Amis and John Wain seemed radical writers in a time when an escape from one's class lay in the open attack on its values. But that assault would not take place until the middle of the 1950s. Positions of influence had to be won, positions now filled by those who had been Oxbridge graduates before the war.

'What happened to that Cambridge crowd?' Michael Straight asked a Cambridge friend, while reporting on the Labour Conference at Blackpool in 1946. 'I don't understand it. We were to have been in power. Lost. Divided. A lost generation.' It was true of the brilliant arts undergraduates of the thirties. They had achieved little or nothing. Some of them had helped in a small way to defeat Fascism, others had helped in a smaller way to betray their country to the Kremlin. But the ideals of the comradeship of Communism in all countries were perverted to the facts of the tyranny of Stalin in Russia and eastern Europe. The dictatorship of the proletariat was a dictatorship, full stop. Those few who still believed in the Soviet system were so compromised by the intelligence which they had provided for it that they were forced into silence about their aid or blackmailed into continuing to serve as moles. Among the dominant Labour Members of Parliament, there were less than a dozen Soviet agents, and these were excluded from all power and security matters by the watchful Clement Attlee, Herbert Morrison and Ernest Bevin. The Cambridge crowd of Michael Straight was a lost generation, its ideals changed by history into a red flare drifting on to an indifferent no man's land in a Cold War.

The discreet Cambridge crowd of the Cavendish and the Kapitsa Club, however, had changed history and were significant in their time. They had changed the course of the war and the future of energy by helping to split the atom and develop nuclear power and radar, cryptography and statistics and computers. They had become the advisers of military machines and governments without having the final say in the use of their discoveries. They were altering the environment of mankind, although they could direct neither the pace nor the course of those alterations. Their applied inventions and their influence were transforming the whole of human society. Cambridge was not only to split the atom, but to aid the computer revolution in Britain. The acts of the Apostles were small change to the constructions of the Cavendish.

9 A Changing of the Guard

The defection of Burgess and Maclean to Russia in 1951 at the point of the discovery of their treachery signalled a replacement of generations, a change of attitudes. Too long the open and self-indulgent conspiracy of the Oxbridge élite in power, too short now the sanctuary of the old school tie. Warned by Anthony Blunt and by the restriction of classified material arriving at the American desk, Maclean and Burgess decided to flee the country. Burgess's last act was typical and damaging. He left a few hundred pounds in bank notes to his young male factotum and a note to say that three of his friends, a peer and a diplomat and Anthony Blunt, would always look after his gay companion. The factotum sold the note for two thousand pounds to the newspapers, which blacked out the three names for fear of libel action, although the London establishment and the secret services knew who they were. It was either another act of that gratuitous carelessness which had always made Burgess seem so improbable a spy, or a calculated final revenge on English society and its cult of friendship by a cunning and spoiled Old Etonian. He may have told his friends that he suffered from a Sir Roger Casement complex, but he fled before he could be punished for betraying his country.

To friends and Russian sympathizers of the thirties such as John Lehmann, the defection was like a small but violent earthquake. It reminded them that the past could strike out at them. A subsidence of earth had taken place without anyone's realizing it. Lehmann himself had seen little of the defectors for some years, but he was told by the novelist Humphrey Slater that he had known Maclean was a Communist agent for some time. His sister, the author Rosamond Lehmann, had also suspected that Burgess was a Soviet spy, trapped in the 'one-way lobster pot' of that conspiratorial role. John Lehmann wrote to Stephen Spender about these informants, and Spender gave the letter to a journalist. The result was a rift between the old literary friends, who felt betrayed by each other as well as by the defectors. The dragon's teeth of time past had sprouted suspicion, fear and investigation.

Burgess's old friend and spy on the Nazis, the Prussian aristocrat Wolfgang zu Puttlitz, had himself returned to East Germany, where his estate had been made into a collective farm. His defection was an inspiration to Burgess, or so Tom Driberg was told. Puttlitz disliked the policy of the western powers in the German Federal Republic. He was convinced that militarism was being born again there to serve against the Soviet Union. 'Everything was being restored that I abhorred,' he declared. 'I decided to get out and go over to the Russians.' In Burgess's case, it was fear of detection that sent him to Moscow with Maclean; but fear of Nazi militarism had helped to make him a Russian spy in the first place. He falsely claimed to Tom Driberg that his going to Russia was like Peter Kapitsa's return:

> You remember when Kapitsa the scientist came back to Russia and a lot of fools said he'd done so under duress, he simply wrote a short letter to *The Times* saying he was a Soviet citizen, etcetera. Well, I wanted to write a short letter to *The Times* saying that, as a Socialist, I had come to a Socialist country to help the cause of peace. But people here were against it.

Not even the Russians believed that Burgess and Maclean had defected from a positive wish to live in Russia. Their defection led to the hunting of other 'moles' within the British establishment. For a while, Philby escaped, although he was dismissed from the intelligence services, obliged to become a newspaper correspondent in Lebanon, and had to flee to Russia himself in his turn. Anthony Blunt was interrogated, but evaded his inquisitors until his denunciation in 1963 by Michael Straight, who also revealed the treachery of Leo Long. Straight had considered exposing his fellow Apostles since 1949, when he had attended an Apostolic dinner in London, had argued fiercely with Eric Hobsbawm about the Communist take-over of Czechoslovakia, and had made it clear to Blunt and to Burgess that he was no longer a believer in the Soviet system. He had thought of denouncing them because Blunt was still in the intelligence service. A year later in Washington, he almost informed the Federal Bureau of Investigation that Burgess was a Soviet spy because the Englishman was now in a position as Second Secretary in the embassy to inform the Kremlin of American troop movements during the Korean War. But the oath of Apostolic secrecy still held. For another thirteen years, Straight would not denounce his fellows in the Cambridge Comintern. When he did, Blunt simply said: 'We always wondered how long it would be before you turned us in.'

A long investigation was begun by the security services, which was intensified after the exposure of Anthony Blunt. Straight went through some two hundred names with British intelligence and identified some twenty-five moles at Cambridge; he estimated that there were eighty moles from all British universities. Forty of the Apostles were investigated, and some fifteen of them were held to have had Communist affiliations and to have passed on intelligence through Blunt and Burgess to the Russians. There was insufficient material, however, to prosecute any of the fifteen suspects. One of them, the leading civil servant, Sir Dennis Proctor, who was close to all government economic decisions for thirty years, was implicated because he was elected an Apostle chronologically between Blunt and Alister Watson, an Admiralty research scientist and an admitted Communist in contact with three Soviet intelligence agents. Proctor was also a close friend of Guy Burgess, which was enough to condemn dozens of distinguished people to the inquiries of the security services. His possible innocence was not helped by Blunt himself when he described Proctor as the best source Burgess ever had for the Russians. Proctor confessed to being a Marxist at Cambridge in the thirties along with hundreds of others, but declared that he had never consciously betrayed his country. 'I had no secrets from Guy Burgess. It is very true. But I had no real secrets to give.'

Through the investigation of Blunt, his close friend, the senior diplomat and Apostle Sir Andrew Cohen, was also implicated. He had behaved heroically when organizing food supplies in Malta during its siege and bombardment in the Second World War. As Governor of Uganda after the war, he had provoked instability by initiating radical land reforms and the deposition of the Kabaka of Buganda. He died early in 1968 of a heart attack before investigations by the security services were complete. A Labour Junior Minister, Bernard Floud, who had probably been recruited as a Soviet agent by James Klugmann at Cambridge, was also implicated by Blunt, and committed suicide after being interrogated.

But these were the old acts of a few of the Apostles and a few at Cambridge. In that secret society of some hundred living members, three were convicted openly as traitors, three were probable traitors, and another twelve of Marxist or homosexual persuasion served as occasional conduits of intelligence to traitors. They were not betrayed by their fellow Apostle, Michael Straight, until years after their treachery was useful to the Russians. Too literally had they proved in their lives the meaning of E. M. Forster's speculative and Apostolic sentence, That it was better to betray one's country than one's friend – only one friend ended by betraying them. In his critique of Anthony Blunt, George Steiner, a founding fellow of Churchill College at Cambridge, asked why Blunt, remained a friend of many top members of the establishment even after he was exposed. There was no answer except in that moral blindness which results from belonging to the same society, club, college, public school or sexual persuasion.

Steiner also wondered how the distinguished art professor Blunt could translate the aesthetic scruples of a pedagogue into the falsehood and forgery of a spy. How could academic integrity have the reverse face of treasonable mendacity? Blunt had commented on the architect Borromini's suicide in 1667, that he had a rare combination of intense emotional power and rational detachment. Blunt seemed to have possessed such a controlled contradiction of character, necessary in a secret agent. He was emotionally attached to his ideology, his homosexuality, and his comrades in arms; he was rationally detached from his country and the murderous consequences of his political actions. Membership of a clandestine élite such as the Apostles, dedicated both to intensely emotional personal relations and to rational discussions and intellectual detachment, only served to deepen the cracks in Blunt's nature. The minor Cambridge tradition of hidden superiority and secret intelligence appealed more to Blunt than its major tradition of the open and passionate pursuit and sharing of knowledge.

As the generation of Cambridge students changed in the early nineteen-fifties, so did the composition of King's and of the Apostles. Its chief architect was Noel Annan, who became Provost of the college after the retirement of J.T.Sheppard and the unexpected death of his successor, an egyptologist. Fewer Old Etonians were accepted by the college, and more grammar school-boys from the north. Marxism was no longer fashionable, but mild Socialism and sociology were. Annan had most of the Labour Party's cabinet to visit and promoted the spread of social studies. The Apostles had recruited one future Labour Minister, Peter Shore, and now included many of the literary editors of the next generation, Ronald Bryden, Karl Miller and John Gross. Annan was conscious of tradition: his most scholarly work was a biography of Leslie Stephen, the father of Virginia Woolf and Vanessa Bell, the link between Cambridge and Bloomsbury. The Arts fellows of King's became Apostles and held high the aesthetic standards of Roger Fry and Anthony Blunt. If Mark Jaffé and Francis Haskell were not as influential as their predecessors, they were respected, and it fell to Jaffé to acquire for the Fitzwilliam Museum after Blunt's death the Poussin sketches and painting which he had treasured.

Tradition ensured also the election of John Cornford's son to the Apostles, as it had of Julian Bell. There were still brilliant Old Etonians chosen for the secret society, particularly Walter Garrison Runciman and Neal Ascherson; but the most brilliant of all were Yale's best scholar, Jan Deutsch, and the protean Jonathan Miller, doctor, comedian and director extraordinary, the polymath of his age. The younger Apostles shared the characteristics which Noel Annan found in the new generation at Cambridge which had replaced the generation of the intellectuals of the thirties. They disliked its amateurism, its complacency, its lack of seriousness, its belief in the supremacy of private life, just as much as they detested the committed, secretive Marxism of that other group of radicals who had reacted from Apostolic and Bloomsbury values before the Second World War. The point was still to change society, but openly through politics and social work, through communications and criticism, using the rigorous scrutiny demanded by the most passionate provincial puritan of them all, F.R.Leavis. The way to overthrow the establishment and replace old values was by the free word, exactly applied in criticism or commentary or satire, not by secret intelligence sneaked to a foreign power in the name of an ideology that had failed.

If Burgess's defection signalled the discarding of some discredited values at King's, the British atomic bomb tests in Australia proved the graveyard of the ideals of the Cavendish physicists. Although sites for nuclear fission tests were offered in the United States under American supervision, the British government decided to conduct its own independent experiments in a Commonwealth country. Supervised by Sir William Penney, the first director of the British Atomic Weapons Research Establishment, a series of atomic bombs were exploded. The first device was loaded into an old frigate and blown up offshore. The British navy feared that the Russians might smuggle a bombship into an English port and detonate it as an atomic Trojan horse. The effects of such an attempt were the object of the test. Unfortunately, a large radioactive cloud was carried by the wind over the Australian mainland, contaminating huge areas. It was the first of some hundred explosions of atomic weapons, three more of which led to fall-out on British aircrews and naval personnel, on Australian towns and on aborigines; some of these soon died. In spite of the known results of fall-out on the Japanese survivors of Hiroshima and Nagasaki, British physicists and scientists allowed the testing of thermonuclear weapons above ground in conditions that led to a deterioration in health and to early deaths of servicemen and civilians.

Scientists working for the government on defence could no longer pretend innocence about the effects of their actions. The weapons they designed would be used, even if they were only tested. They did not warn the military well enough about the probable dire consequences of detonating nuclear weapons. And although they became more important as advisers to governments and general staffs, they would still claim that they had hardly any influence on the employment of their inventions. The more responsible physicists did do something to put pressure on all their governments to cease trying out nuclear weapons in the atmosphere, which could carry clouds of pollution world-wide. But although Solly Zuckerman would see the radical young members of the Tots and Quots now being ennobled and becoming part of a new establishment, he did not see any major Cabinet Minister or general or admiral come from a scientific background. Operational research may have been significantly a creation of the Tots and Quots, who had also campaigned for the appointment of specialist advisers to government departments, but those scientific peers and advisers did not have the power to change the decisions of their governments. Their terrible inventions were not under their control. And although they had made these Golems, they would take no responsibility for the use of what they had wrought.

In his criticism of C.P.Snow's lecture on 'Two Cultures', the distinguished scientist Michael Yudkin declared that government ministers probably never properly understood the hazards of nuclear tests. They could not evaluate scientific evidence because they were not trained scientists. Thus they had to rely on the opinions of their advisers, who usually stated their views with more dogmatism than the evidence warranted. The specialist advisers themselves might distort or fail to mention evidence that might prejudice a chosen policy. The ethics of the Cavendish were often mute in the corridors of Whitehall.

If the splitting of the atom at the Cavendish had finally led to a secret of causing mass death, it also led to a secret of all life. Sir Lawrence Bragg, a founder of crystallography, had become the director of the Cambridge laboratory. He was particularly interested in solving the structures of proteins, then thought to contain the genes which transmitted hereditary traits. But recent research in New York had suggested that deoxyribonucleic acid or DNA molecules might be the carriers of genetic material.

In 1951, a young American biologist James D. Watson came to the Cavendish to work on the structure of proteins in a unit led by the Austrian émigré chemist, Max Perutz. He soon developed a partnership with the brilliant and temperamental physicist Francis Crick, who Watson said was never in a modest mood, even if he might one day be considered a Rutherford or a Bohr. Using the patient work of the London physicist Maurice Wilkins on the DNA molecule, Watson and Crick began to speculate on the genetic origins of life. The great American chemist Linus Pauling was also experimenting in California. Three groups were competing to discover the primary secret of human biology, a discovery which would be as momentous as splitting the atom. The front runner Wilkins would be a loser. As Watson observed, Wilkins had escaped into biology only to find it as unpleasant 'as physics, with its atomic consequences'.

There were important differences in understanding between biologists and geneticists, chemists and crystallographers and physicists. The Cavendish unit managed to bridge these gaps. Using the shape of a double helix, the form that Leonardo da Vinci himself had created in his staircase at the château of Chambord, Watson and Crick solved the problem of the structure of the DNA molecule. In a letter written from the Cavendish on 12 March 1953, Watson outlined the discovery in crude diagrams. It was the beginning of all genetic engineering and the biochemical changing of human society, twenty-one years after nuclear fission at Cambridge, eight years after the dropping of the atomic bomb on Hiroshima, simultaneous with the making of hydrogen bombs and the poisoning of the atmosphere with radioactive fall-out.

As Percy Bysshe Shelley wrote of the west wind, so the Cavendish was destroyer and preserver. Even the finding of the structure of the genes could have terrible consequences. Since fundamental changes in the shape of living things could now be developed, Mary Shelley's fantasy of Frankenstein approached reality. We could not only alter the plants and animals of the earth, but also ourselves. James D. Watson himself was horrified by the probability of cloning, the reproduction of identical human beings. Great controversies and legal measures arose about scientific meddling with ordinary human reproduction. Sperm could be frozen and banked, babies conceived in test-tubes. We could, indeed, begin to remake ourselves, for better or for worse.

10 O Yes - My Country, White and Wrong

from *That Was the Week that Was*

The fathers of the Oxbridge students of the fifties had fought the 'last just war' against Fascism. Their children, seeking to define their own generation, looked for a just cause. In eating their sour grapes, they were reversing the original, to set their fathers' teeth on edge. Their rebellion could not have the certainties of the Communism of the thirties, now tainted by Stalin's genocidal crimes of the Gulag and the expansion of Soviet neo-imperialism over eastern Europe. But there could be a revolt of manners, of taste, of style, expressed in comedy, satire, drama and polemic. And if the children seized the means of communication, their messages would be heard.

A political crisis supplied the occasion for protest, a human reaction provided the Just Cause. The British invasion of the Suez Canal Zone and the Russian invasion of Hungary in 1956 signalled the realities of power, which were exposed by its application. The campaign against the manufacture and testing of nuclear weapons, which began at Easter two years later sponsored by the veteran pacifist Bertrand Russell, was the first major protest movement outside parliament since the hunger marches of the 1930s. These were revulsions from a government policy that clung to colonial possessions and licensed the manufacture of the hydrogen bomb. Both provided the catch-all of apparent political truths that had motivated the Socialists of the thirties, except that the new movement was of opposition, not of commitment. The enemy was the same, that establishment of older men who pursued antiquated

and destructive policies: the very word 'establishment' was resur-
rected in the *Spectator* to condemn the official concealment of the
connections of Burgess and Maclean before their defection to Russia.
The current bogies were class privilege, colonialism and censorship;
the Bastille to be stormed was the system of promotion, by which
the establishment staffed itself only from those who respected it.
There was no ultimate faith such as Marxism. How could there
be, when Russian tanks had suppressed the workers and students
in Budapest?

The Civil War in Spain had been the opposite case: then Russian
tanks had defended the Republic against Fascism. There was no
just war possible now, not with western imperialism joined by eastern imperialism, confronting each other with nuclear weapons that
might destroy all humanity. For such radicals as Jack Haldane,
the Suez intervention was a golden opportunity to justify a planned
emigration to a job in India with the claim that he did not wish
to live in a criminal country that had attacked Egypt. 'I want to
live in a free country,' he declared at London airport for the benefit
of American reporters, 'where there are no foreign troops based
all over the place.'

The Suez expedition was a major one, even more futile than
the Duke of York's famous sortie when he marched ten thousand
men to the top of a hill and then down again. A huge armada
was cobbled together, one hundred and fifty warships and eighty
thousand men. Through moral and political scruples, the British
government delayed its assault on the Canal Zone and lied about
its intentions. Israeli armies were already doing the dirty work and
destroying Egyptian forces. When the British attack was finally
launched on the pretext of stopping the local war, it was too late.
Under Russian threats of possible nuclear retaliation and American
refusal to support the adventure, the British halted the operations
and withdrew their forces. Their French allies were forced to follow
suit. It had been better not to have launched the invasion or to
have completed it successfully. The worst result was a half-cocked
intervention that ended in a complete fiasco. The failure proved
that there were only two great powers in the world. Without the
support of one of them, nothing much could be done.

During the time of the Suez crisis, Cambridge was deeply divided. Hundreds of students went to join in the anti-government rally in Trafalgar Square. A few left to fall fighting in Hungary or to bring relief to the refugees on the Austrian borders. Still fewer refused to be called back to the army as reservists for the purpose of invading Egypt. Emotionally, the Russian assault on a European country was more devastating to radical thought than the British attack on a canal in the eastern Mediterranean. 'I cared more about Hungary,' the novelist Margaret Drabble said before going up to Newnham College. 'The Empire had better go, anyway.'

The consequence of Suez was, indeed, that the empire went, under the astute direction of the new British Prime Minister, Harold Macmillan. The winds of change that he released to blow across the last of the British colonies confirmed the doldrums of the Suez invasion. America and Russia were the only great powers now: yet the new Conservative defence policy of increased reliance on nuclear weapons stimulated the just cause of the Campaign for Nuclear Disarmament, which concluded at another Trafalgar Square rally an annual march of forty miles from the Atomic Weapons Research centre at Aldermaston. Although the government hardly altered because of the Suez débâcle or the CND marches, a process of change was begun. The children of the 'last just war' were breaking down the gates of the establishment.

A new élite was being processed at Cambridge, which demanded its share of power in a hurry. No one could express that change of generations better than John Cornford's son, James, who studied history at Trinity College, became an Apostle, then a lecturer in politics at Edinburgh University, and finally the head of the Nuffield Foundation in London. He reacted from the cult based on his father: he went back to the classical and liberal academic tradition of his Cambridge family: his grandfather had been a great friend of Bertrand Russell and William Morris. He called his father John 'the apologia for his generation' – an honest militant Communist while the other Communists among the Apostles were covert spies, hiding behind their heroic martyr in Spain. James Cornford himself was an agnostic, who did not believe in the simplicities of Communism. He was against making a gesture during the crisis of Suez and

Hungary. 'What if the gesture is for oneself?' But all the same, he reckoned that the crisis 'knocked the bounce out of our lot', which opted for scepticism and milk-and-water Socialism. He considered the older Apostles to be at a low tide, relying on personal friendships, without intellectual rigour. After all, what was there to believe?

For future critics and teachers of English literature, there were the beliefs of F.R.Leavis and his methods of inquiry, expressed with vehemence and conviction from his bunker in Downing College. He was never fashionable, always at war with the faculty. His was an ideology with a narrow canon of approved reading. As the poet and critic Donald Davie wrote, his prophet was Leavis, whose magazine *Scrutiny* was a bible:

> To be a member of what Leavis promoted as 'a minority culture' one had to be indeed a precisian in speech and, for the most part, in manners also; one had to cultivate a propriety of culture which meant necessarily, so the doctrine went, propriety of morals; one had to be a didactic person; and one had to be prepared for others to be affronted, or bored, by one's pretensions.

As a former disciple of Leavis, Donald Davie could enter imaginatively into the mind of the fanatic and the revolutionary, the commissar or the gauleiter. He understood the appeal of Communism or Fascism through having a body of scriptural texts for reference, through feeling one of a band of embattled brothers, through seeing ruthlessness and blind obedience as virtues. A Cambridge student both before and after the Second World War, Davie himself could never take to the rival psychological security of Communism. 'My generation came up to the university in the time of the Molotov–Ribbentrop pact; thus there was no excuse for us if we were starry-eyed about the Stalinist left.'

It was Leavis's commitment to literature that made him so attractive a figure to the poet Thom Gunn, to the critic Karl Miller, and even to the economist John Vaizey, who saw Leavis as the representative of Cambridge's main contribution to the tone of intellectual life: a ruthless, forthright intellectual honesty, exemplified by the puritan revolution. This necessity to bare feelings, to analyse motives, to tell the truth at all costs had its dangers, particularly in personal relations. 'It was like meeting an evangelist,' the director Trevor Nunn said of Leavis, '– you come out of the crowd and offer yourself.'

The shock of Leavis extended even to the Apostles, who were reforming and renewing their commitment to the old Cambridge tradition. Scrutiny, analysis, and telling the truth wittily had always been part of the meetings of the secret society, but the influence of G. E. Moore and his misinterpreters had made the group a narcissistic sodality that pursued personal fulfilment and gratification. The Communist reaction of the thirties within the Apostles was replaced by a puritan and rigorous return to old Apostolic and university values and traditions, allied with a deliberate professionalism in pursuing a career. Heterosexuality replaced homosexuality.

The scandals within the society were no longer a question of Lytton Strachey's going off with Maynard Keynes's boy-friend, or vice versa. They were of one Apostle taking away another Apostle's wife and marrying her, or of two Apostles sharing a wife and becoming bitter enemies. The years of close male companionship were over. And if E. M. Forster would still read chapters from his unpublished homosexual novel *Maurice* to favoured undergraduates, he was an elegant anachronism of exaggerated modesty in a clandestine group that was changing with the times.

Karl Miller, a favoured pupil of Leavis at Downing College, was an exemplar of that change. A scholar from the Royal High School at Edinburgh, he became determinedly proletarian in attitude as a reaction from his National Service in the Royal Engineers. With his friends, he joined or rejoined the working class, 'dressing in rough textures and dark, dangerous shades, and looking more like displaced persons than spruce mechanics'. To them, social mobility was another name for snobbery, yet Miller certainly became socially mobile enough. He stayed on at Cambridge to do postgraduate work and join the new breed of Apostles before leaving for the Treasury, then for a career in television, and then to serve as the most influential literary editor of his age. Alternating with or succeeding a fellow Apostle, Ronald Bryden, Miller became the arbiter of the book pages of the *Spectator*, the *New Statesman*, and the *Listener*. He then broke into fresh print as the London editor of the *New*

York Review of Books, followed by founding the *London Review of Books*, at the same time as another Apostle John Gross who had succeeded him at the *New Statesman* was then editing the established *Times Literary Supplement*.

While editor of the *Times Literary Supplement*, Gross acted in a most un-Apostolic way. He broke a long tradition by making the unknown reviewers sign their reviews. Secrecy seemed no longer good policy. 'Everyone must confess that there is a dangerous temptation, and an unmanly security, an unfair advantage in concealment,' he wrote of his anonymous reviewers. While a highwayman might wear a mask, 'a man that goes about an honest errand does not want it and will disdain to wear it'. Yet Gross continued to wear his mask as an Apostle and finally went on to help edit the book pages of the *New York Times*. His rival editor Karl Miller was unexpectedly appointed, despite little academic experience, to one of the three top chairs in the country, as Lord Northcliffe Professor of Modern English at University College, London. It was a triumph of ability and acquaintance over formal qualifications.

John Vaizey had also declared that a significant consequence of Cambridge was a complex network of acquaintance and shared experience without which he would never have escaped the back streets of his birth to rise to professorships in Economics and to the House of Lords. While there is no 'Cambridge Mafia' that is a political or communications group in Britain, the existence of the Apostles still makes them suspected of being a secret society that favours its own members and helps to secure them positions of influence. In fact, Vaizey was correct, and only a complex network of wide relationships and shared experience well outside the confines of college or club can explain the later success of many Cambridge graduates in the fields of communications, politics and academics, and particularly in scientific areas. For instance, the present directors of the National Theatre and the Royal Shakespeare Company, Sir Peter Hall and Trevor Nunn, owe nothing to the Apostles, something to F.R. Leavis, and much to the theatrical groups at Cambridge, the Marlowe Society in particular. The only reason that the Apostles are considered a conspiracy is that they take an oath of clandestinity in contradiction to the principles of the university which tolerates them. They are not a cabinet, they are not a business, they are not an intelligence service, they are not a masonic lodge. They will always be misunderstood as long as they cling to the unmanly security from which John Gross liberated his literary reviewers.

The other exemplar of Apostolic change in the fifties was Jonathan Miller, no relation of Karl Miller, although they married two sisters. Jonathan's father was a leading London psychoanalyst, and he studied medicine at Cambridge, although he had a passionate interest in linguistic philosophy, particularly in Wittgenstein and G. E. Moore. It was Miller's satire on Moore and his apples in the revue *Beyond the Fringe* that showed just how much the younger Apostles repudiated the values of the older ones. Jonathan became the most brilliant figure of his time, an intuitive diagnostician, superlative in conversation and mimicry, an inventive comedian and an iconoclastic director of theatre and opera, a man of every talent who was master of all the trades in which he chose to perform except the cinema. His success owed nothing to his connections. Above all, he represented the professionalism of his generation of Cambridge graduates, whether Apostles or not, who took their place so easily in the performing arts and communications system of their country.

Jonathan Miller himself always despised the word 'satirist', so much used to describe him and the many other Oxbridge graduates who were to mock and attack received opinion and old values in *Beyond the Fringe*, The Establishment, *That Was the Week that Was, Cambridge Circus, The Goodies*, and *Monty Python*. To Bamber Gascoigne, the author of one of the first Cambridge revues to transfer to London, his contemporaries thought of themselves as spearheading a revolution. 'In our own way we were, in the sense of helping to get rid of what had gone before. But it wasn't a revolution that would lead anywhere. Kerensky's rather than Lenin's.' Although revue performers and comedians were relentlessly thrown up by Oxbridge for the next fifteen years – a case for the Equal Opportunities Commission in Gascoigne's opinion – their opportunity to perform, particularly on television, was the consequence of the more important breed of producers, directors and presenters, who also left Oxbridge in the fifties for jobs in television, broadcasting and other communications industries. Where they did not know one another, they knew of one another. The list is legion, from Jeremy Isaacs to Graeme MacDonald to Michael Deakin, from Peter Jay to David Frost to John Tusa, *ad infinitum*. In the delta of the media flow the waters of the Isis and the Cam.

The formation, as Raymond Williams observed, moved through; but satire could not change the world. 'After twenty years of mocking impersonation we are stuck with public figures even more ludicrous than any of the original targets.' Gascoigne's revolutionaries of the fifties were capable of replacing the establishment, but only with its likenesses or with themselves. Those who were actually changing human society were, as usual, unseen and hardly heard. Curiously enough, the just cause of nuclear disarmament served as another chance for the arts graduates to attack the scientists and technologists who had invented the monstrous atomic weaponry. The new Doctor Frankenstein was to be Stanley Kubrick's *Doctor Strangelove*, subtitled 'How I Learned to Stop Worrying and Love the Bomb'. The original atomic fission had been performed in the Cavendish Laboratory, and the literary puritans of Downing College did not allow the physicists to forget it. Their attack was on the Cavendish's chief interpreter and only major novelist, C.P.Snow, a founding fellow of Cambridge's new scientific foundation Churchill College; its Master had been the leader of British atomic research, Sir John Cockcroft. By attacking Snow and denying his premise of the 'two cultures', F.R.Leavis only proved that the 'two cultures' were more antagonistic than ever.

In a memorial lecture at Cambridge in 1959, C.P.Snow made some simple, but important statements that reflected on his experience and widely influenced his time. By training he was a scientist; by vocation, a writer. He had a ringside view of one of the most creative periods in all physics. He had intimate friends among scientists and writers, but they kept apart. He called their different little societies 'two cultures'. To him, 'culture' meant a development of the mind; also anthropologically, a group living in the same environment, linked by common habits and assumptions and way of life. He thought that the literary cultures of Chelsea and Greenwich

Village shared a common language, but to them, the scientists at the Massachusetts Institute of Technology talked Tibetan. The intellectual and practical life of the whole of western society was being split. As far as the new scientific revolution was concerned, literary intellectuals were 'natural Luddites'.

Exaggerating his case, Snow dismissed most leading writers of the nineteenth and twentieth centuries as pessimists without the social hope of the scientists, who had the future in their bones. Snow here equated literary culture with 'traditional culture', which did not wish the future to exist. The gap between these two cultures, scientific and literary-traditional, was growing wider in England, where there was early educational specialization and where social forms were crystallized. In Victorian times, Lord Salisbury had his own laboratory at Hatfield, the Prime Minister Arthur Balfour was interested in natural science, and the leading civil servant, Sir John Anderson, had done research in inorganic chemistry at Leipzig. 'None of that degree of interchange at the top of the Establishment is likely, or indeed, thinkable, now.'

The separation between the scientists and the non-scientists was greater than ever. Academics at Cambridge had ignored the industrial revolution, which had enriched them and had separated Disraeli's Two Nations into Snow's Two Cultures. Yet even more significant was the new scientific revolution which Snow dated from the thirties and the use of atomic particles in industry, largely the creation of the Cavendish Laboratory. The innovative industrial society of electronics, atomic energy and automation would make society cardinally different and enable the western nations not only to benefit their own populations but also bridge the abyss between the rich and the poor nations by exporting their technology. The danger lay in the split of the two cultures both at the universities and in the government, by which the scientists who managed the new revolution could not communicate their social hope to the administrators. Time was running out for western societies to close the gap between their cultures. History was merciless to failure, nor would we in the west write it.

Snow's plain language and simple dialectic appealed world-wide. Yet it provoked a vicious assault at Cambridge from the self-elected guardian of the university's essential values, F.R.Leavis. As provincial and rigorous and condemnatory as any regicide in the Civil War, Leavis hated Snow for his international success, his loose definitions, and even his literary reputation. To Leavis, Snow was portentously ignorant, but a portent of an ignorant time in which he was considered a sage and a master-mind.

At another memorial lecture in 1962, attended by a crowd of hundreds of undergraduates and dons, Leavis claimed that he was not enjoying his slaughterous field-day. In fact, his words breathed envy; his tongue was malice incarnate. He demeaned the university traditions that he claimed to be defending. He talked of Snow as an intellectual nullity, as undistinguished as it was possible to be, incapable of posing or answering problems. As a novelist, let alone as a scientist or a thinker, Snow did not exist. In Snow's major novel, *The Affair*, science was a mere word, the vocation merely postulated. Snow's lecture on the 'Two Cultures' was a document in the study of the cliché. Snow was as ignorant of history as of literature. Leavis used the minor tools of a Wittgenstein to brand Snow's statement about scientists having the future in their bones as not a meaningful proposition; he forgot that most of his vilifications of Snow were meaningless too. He rightly pointed out that Snow had not defined 'culture' exactly and had slid from 'literary' to 'traditional culture', as well as dismissing the worth of the major literary figures of the previous hundred and fifty years.

Leavis concluded in vainglory. He was not a Luddite. Human intelligence was needed to respond to the challenges of the new technology. The proper study of Cambridge was language. The centre of the university should be a vital English school. Twenty years of running the critical magazine *Scrutiny* had taught him that the academic was the enemy and the academic could be beaten. He and his disciples were, and knew they were, Cambridge, 'the essential Cambridge in spite of Cambridge'.

This rancorous attack signalled not only the division of the 'two cultures', but also the split in the values of the old and the new Cambridge. As much as he was condemning the significance of the scientific pre-eminence claimed by Snow, Leavis was attacking the old Apostolic pursuit of self-gratification and style, which still informed much of the Cambridge English department and the London literary reviews. Ironically enough, many of the younger Apostles who were becoming the new literary editors were profoundly influenced by Leavis and by his teachings. On the whole, they were the very puritanical and provincial professionals that he liked his students to be. But in this worst display of his vindictive and righteous self-justification, Leavis proved that he could scrutinize the faults of every leading figure but not his own.

The most just of the comments on the controversy that so acutely exposed the many little rival 'cultures' and traditions at Cambridge was written by a research biochemist, Michael Yudkin, for the *Cambridge Review*. Although praised by Leavis for denigrating the use of the phrase 'two cultures' when there were many 'cultures', Yudkin agreed with two of Snow's theses. There was a failure of contact between scientists and non-scientists. This failure was unfortunate and probably dangerous. But Yudkin did not think any significant improvement was possible. With his claim that society's hope now lay with the scientists, Snow was pursuing the falsely optimistic idea of an age of Leonardo da Vincis. There would be no bridge across the gap between science and the arts. There would only be the atrophy of Snow's traditional culture, which would be gradually annexed by the scientific one until only a single culture remained. In his last words on this commentary, Snow seemed to accept some of Yudkin's criticism and pessimism, saying Renaissance man was no longer possible; England had lost even the pretence of a common culture.

The scientists were no Dr Strangeloves. The best of them, particularly at Cambridge, did try to stop the pernicious fall-out from the testing of nuclear weapons in the atmosphere. As Sir Peter Medawar wrote, scientists feared the effect of radiation on genetic materials; but 'a principal social function of science is to act as scapegoat for blunders and malfunctions of its political masters'. Scientific contacts between Britain and Russia did improve, in spite of the Suez crisis, with the emergence of Khrushchev as the Soviet leader. A distinguished Soviet delegation of scientists visited the atomic research centre at Harwell in 1957, and the following year, Cockcroft returned to Russia to visit its Institute of Atomic Energy and its Nuclear Physics Research laboratory at Dubna outside Moscow. He was escorted by Kurchatov and met again by his friend, Kapitsa. He even had an interview with Khrushchev himself and requested that Kapitsa should be allowed to come to England, where he would be quite safe and from where he would be returned to Russia. Khrushchev joked about the matter, but was serious about the necessity for talks on nuclear disarmament. With his views on the importance of science in government, Cockcroft was particularly impressed that both Kapitsa and Kurchatov had direct government telephone lines to Khrushchev at the Kremlin.

The old Cambridge Apostle Bertrand Russell had first suggested international conferences on science and world affairs in a manifesto drafted in December 1954. The declaration was signed by Einstein shortly before his death, and by other leading scientists. Cockcroft supported the idea and began representations, which were to lead to the first of many Pugwash conferences; at them, experts from both east and west sat down to exchange information and differences. It was at these early Pugwash meetings that the conditions for the Partial Nuclear Test Ban Treaty of 1963 between Russia, America and Britain were unofficially established. In Churchill's famous phrase, jaw-jaw was always better than war-war.

It was high time to reach a limited agreement. After the débâcle of Suez, the British government followed the American example in moving from an expensive conventional defence policy towards a cheaper one of massive deterrence. Fewer armies and navies, more nuclear weapons and means to deliver them. It may have been true, as one officer at Suez remarked, that an H-bomb could not keep the canal open, but a strategy of deterrence based on the new hydrogen bombs allowed the British government to cut down its army by a third, to end military conscription, and to reduce its defence spending from eleven to seven per cent of its gross national product.

Sir Anthony Eden had been wrong as Prime Minister about the consequences of the Suez adventure. He was also to prove wrong about placing too heavy a reliance on nuclear weapons at the expense of conventional forces. 'If continents, and not merely small islands,' he wrote, 'were doomed to destruction, all are equal on the grim reckoning.' They were not equal in the smaller wars short of nuclear war, as the Suez crisis proved. But the possession of the hydrogen bomb gave Britain the status of a great power, even if she had not the resources to support her pretensions.

For good or ill, Britain persisted in the pursuit of independence through nuclear deterrence. But nuclear power could not change British society by itself, nor finally preserve it. The well-being of the country depended on an economic revolution based on scientific invention, not on a military solution. If C.P.Snow exaggerated the gap between the 'two cultures', he was correct that electronics, the peaceful use of atomic energy, and automation would make society radically different. Inventions in electronics would spawn the computer revolution, which would make Cambridge itself the Silicon Fen of England, with Sir Clive Sinclair and his competitors setting up shop around the abilities of the scientists of the ancient university. Atomic energy may still be the force that keeps the perilous peace between the great powers, but more beneficially, it supplies the electric grids of nations short of less dangerous fuels. The arms race of deterrent weapons still continues in successive escalations. In 1957, the Russians put into operation the first intercontinental ballistic missile and sent up the first sputnik into the heavens, creating a 'technological Pearl Harbor' for the Americans, who quickly riposted with their own missiles and spacecraft. To protect themselves militarily and economically, all governments with the necessary technological expertise pushed forward with new defence systems and industrial innovations at whatever cost to existing societies.

The third industrial revolution had begun and it had begun largely at Cambridge. C.P.Snow had not even mentioned in his lecture on the 'two cultures' the radical genetic engineering that evolved from the discovery of the double helix in the DNA molecule, even though that discovery had been made by Francis Crick, another founding fellow of Churchill College. The third industrial revolution that the Cavendish had helped to start was so awesome in its application that no literary Apostle, no arts professor, no master of the media, and certainly no politician could gauge its consequences or adequately describe its future.

11 Just to be on the Safe Side

At a meeting between Harold Macmillan and President John F.Kennedy, the British Prime Minister asked his nuclear expert, Sir William Penney, how many hydrogen bombs would be needed to finish off Britain. 'Five, I should think, Prime Minister,' Penney said, then added: 'Just to be on the safe side, let's say eight.'

This safety factor allowed for a narrow margin of error in British foreign policy. A reliance on atomic weapons was an illusion. Although a balance of nuclear deterrence created a common interest between the United States of America and Soviet Russia because they would be the chief victims of a total war, minor powers with a nuclear strike capacity only held wild cards in the international great game. The independent atomic weapons of Britain and France were classified as additions to the American arsenal by the Russians, while Chinese atomic weapons represented a threat which the Russians thought was directed against themselves after their split with the various Beijing regimes. By the 1980s, many minor nations possessed or had the capacity to make nuclear weapons, led by Israel and South Africa, and followed by India, Pakistan, Iraq and Argentina. Proliferation was the danger to world peace, a minor power or a terrorist organization using a nuclear weapon in a local war. The atomic fission started at the Cavendish Laboratory had split open a box of mass destruction. Its last hope of control lay in the imposition by both superpowers of a stalemate on their own deployment of the weapons and in their laying an embargo on the production of nuclear materials and weaponry elsewhere, even by their allies. Dual possession of the final solution by Russia and America might prevent the outbreak of a Third World War as it had for forty years, but it was a game that only two should play. The 'Big Five' powers that officially had atomic weapons were already three too many in the diplomacy of nuclear deterrence.

The Cambridge physicists knew that, as did most of the world's scientists. They sought through the Pugwash conferences and later through the Erice meetings in Sicily to advise the superpowers on nuclear disarmament and on measures to prevent proliferation. They were not successful. They had given their governments the means of utter destruction, but they were not allowed to provide the means of controlling it. They could not put the lid back on the Cavendish box of atomic tricks. The military increasingly controlled the possible use of nuclear weapons in the United States and in Russia. There was, indeed, not only a growth in all countries of Eisenhower's military-industrial complex, but the rise of a military-scientific establishment in America and Britain, following the example of the Soviet Union, where Peter Kapitsa had been the exemplar of the use of academic research by the state for the purposes of armament.

In Russia, Kapitsa remained a respected figure, but of waning influence. He represented the official 'independence' of Soviet scientists. He might urge at the Academy in 1964 that the directors of scientific institutes should be allowed more discretion in recruitment and more flexibility in the allocation of resources to research; but his plea fell on deaf ears. The Russian Communist Party and state allocated all scientific resources and mostly for military purposes. Kapitsa himself was allowed to visit his old friend Cockcroft at Cambridge in 1966 before their deaths; at dinner at Trinity College, he still found his black academic gown waiting for him. He received the Rutherford Medal of the British Institute of Physics and delivered a lecture on Rutherford to the Royal Society, presided over by Patrick Blackett, by this time a member of the House of Lords and the Labour government's adviser on the new Ministry of Technology. Kapitsa knew that he and his old Cavendish associates could not harness the nuclear forces which they had unleashed. The state ruled everywhere, and the state only nodded at their advice, and allocated funds where these benefited state policy. As Kapitsa said:

The year that Rutherford died there disappeared for ever the happy days of free scientific work which gave us such delight in our youth. Science has lost her freedom. Science has become a productive force. She has become rich but she has become enslaved and part of her is veiled in secrecy.

Kapitsa was correct. Science was now considered a productive force, was richer and more enslaved, and was certainly veiled in secrecy. The new Labour government tried to recruit Sir John Cockcroft as a Minister of State and chief adviser to the Ministry of Defence, but he refused to neglect his duties as Master of Churchill College. The military correspondent of *The Times* took the job and was ennobled as Lord Chalfont; he was soon joined in the House of Lords by another scientific adviser to the government, Solly Zuckerman, who had also refused Chalfont's post as Minister of State. Both Cockcroft and Zuckerman knew of the increasing inability of leading scientists to influence governments on disarmament, on international relations, or on the allocation of funds to 'pure' research in science.

Cockcroft himself died of a heart attack at the end of an incident that put strain on Anglo–Soviet diplomacy. He had invited a young protégé of Kapitsa, Vladimir Tkachenko, to study low-temperature physics at Churchill College. Tkachenko was abducted by officials from the Russian embassy and rescued by Special Branch policemen at London airport from an aeroplane bound for Moscow. He was then judged to be suffering from a mental breakdown and was allowed to return to Russia. Cockcroft's sad death at the time of the incident allowed Kapitsa to pay tribute to him as a promoter of peace and international collaboration. 'It was my privilege together with Sir John to bring closer the scientists of our two countries.'

In spite of attempts at collaboration between the older scientists, American and some western governments became more determined to curtail the free flow of research information and technological innovation. The era of Rutherford's Cavendish with its open international exchange of scientific intelligence was terminated for ever. Although there was trade in research findings in fields without a direct military application, there were more and more efforts to contain the spread of any invention. Without question, the strength of the western economies lay in their advanced technology. As with atomic secrets, it was cheaper and quicker for eastern bloc countries to acquire that technology by trade or espionage than to fund similar research projects at home. While much trade between the east and the west was legitimate, some was an excuse for the transfer of technology. Successive American administrations prodded western European governments to control or to ban the trade in strategic exports, particularly in the field of high technology. With missiles and weaponry increasingly dependent on computers and micro-chips, the Americans could argue that such exports had a military application. One recent American study showed that the export to Russia of computer equipment, recently restricted, would have saved the Soviet military budget thirteen billion dollars over the life span of the technology and would have cost the west fourteen billion dollars to offset the Soviet gain. Richard Perle, the Assistant Secretary of Defence, stated that the countries of eastern Europe had saved more than fifty billion dollars in costs for research and development on their new weapons by stealing western innovations. Industrial espionage had become the leading form of spying, with minimal costs and great benefits.

American efforts to restrain trade to the east fell foul of two important groups; businessmen and those academics who were economists or scientists. The Labour governments of the 1960s strongly encouraged trade with the Soviet bloc. The Prime Minister, Harold Wilson, ennobled leading traders with the east; Rudy Sternberg as Lord Plurenden; and the mackintosh manufacturer Lord Kagan. Wilson also put in the House of Lords two radical economists from Central Europe, Cambridge's Lord Kaldor and Oxford's Lord Balogh, of whom it was said at Balliol that there were 'three kinds of conversation – dialogue, monologue and Balogh'. In 1968, an Anglo-Russian agreement for co-operation in the fields of applied science was signed, followed by the creation of the International Technological Collaboration Unit, set up in a British atomic energy establishment to answer questions on nuclear research from countries abroad. By the end of the

Wilson administrations, the United States of America had returned
to its position under the Macmahon Act of 1946 and was refusing
to share advances in nuclear research with allied scientists. The
open transfer of technology to the east had made Britain appear
a security risk.

Increasing efforts by American administrations to embargo computer exports – recently given the code name of Operation Exodus
– seemed to British scientists to be a threat to their personal and
academic freedom. The area of material that was defined as 'militarily sensitive' had become so wide that it included nearly all areas
of research into communications. As most advanced computers used
American components, the breach of the embargo on exports could
lead to punitive judgements *in absentia* in American courts. Rutherford's ideals at the Cavendish could not survive in an age of scientific
research funded by the government and directed towards the interests of the state. To its great embarrassment, the United States
even had to proceed against friends of Israel for smuggling krytons
there, electronic switches that might be used to trigger nuclear
weapons. Friend or enemy, in time of peace as well as war, a foreign
power was banned from receiving all strategic materials. Those
who provided such goods were spies, not exchangers of legitimate
intelligence and information.

'Can Athens hold off Sparta without becoming its mirror image?'
The question is asked in an age when science has put an exponential
increase in power in the hands of the governing élites of the modern
nation state. Scientists cannot control the powers that they have
given to the governors. They do not govern the governors. The
powers that they have given the governors erode and destroy the
freedoms and principles that nurture scientific discovery. By engaging in certain fields of research, scientists are turned willy-nilly
into agents of the government or the military. By exchanging information with scientists abroad, they may unwittingly become foreign
agents and appear to be spies. Now Spartan rules dictate to
Athenian ideals, and the Cam flows into the Tiber.

Unfortunately, Cambridge and its élite had become associated
with espionage rather than with its traditional values of integrity
and inquiry. It was ironical that a university, which had sent out

so many of its privileged classes to die in the First World War, should be accused of fostering traitors during the Second World War. The sins of some of the Apostles and their Communist associates tarnished the considerable contributions of Cambridge scientists to the war effort and towards a new industrial revolution, as well as the perennial commitment of most of the dons and undergraduates to an open and democratic society and to the pursuit of knowledge, to be used for the benefit of all. Unfortunately again, the Cambridge spies of the thirties all appeared to be the sons of privileged fathers and to be educated at private schools. So the discovery of their espionage was followed by an attack on the establishment, which had allowed the traitors access and development within it. As some Apostles, old Etonians, diplomats and civil servants were traitors, so their whole society of privilege appeared rotten and ripe for replacement. The worm in the bud spoilt the whole flower of England. The classes that had died for their country appeared to be those who ruled in order to betray it.

Yet the power of the members of that education and that class continued. David Caute in *The Fellow Travellers* estimated that the defections of the traitors led to more severe security measures in the defence and atomic energy sections of the establishment, and in the diplomatic service. Of 120,000 people who were interviewed, only 163 civil servants faced tribunals. Of these, one-fifth were reinstated and half were transferred to posts that did not involve security. There was little change at the top, and not much more room.

The other traitors did not serve prison sentences. After co-operating with the security services, Cairncross was allowed to live in exile in Italy. Leo Long confessed from retirement, but was not judged worthy of punishment. Other suspected traitors died before they were brought to book. Philby continued his intrigues and took Maclean's wife off his comrade in Moscow. Vodka was the main solace of the three leading male English defectors to Russia, especially in the mouth of Burgess, whose drunken days were sympathetically shown by Alan Bennett in his play, *An Englishman Abroad*. It was the view of the sceptical generation of the fifties looking back at the corrupt generation of the thirties. Snobbery was a great part of treachery, Bennett knew that; but his age had come to restore the values of the establishment, not to undermine it.

One Apostle, however, lost his title. Anthony Blunt had been knighted by the Queen for his distinguished services as the Surveyor of the Queen's Pictures. When, later, he was publicly exposed, the Queen stripped him of his knighthood. No one had been so disgraced since Sir Roger Casement, who also had his knighthood removed before he was executed as a traitor during the First World War. Trinity College also took away from Blunt his honorary fellowship. This exceptional action by a Cambridge College had also happened during the First World War, when another Apostle Bertrand Russell had lost his lectureship at Trinity for opposing the war. Blunt did not serve any time in prison, but died some years after his exposure by his fellow Apostle Michael Straight, who had broken the oaths of secrecy of that exclusive society. Straight did not visit Cambridge again. He thought his actions as an informer would make his fellow Apostles angry.

There were social changes taking place in Britain as well as a change of generations. The rise of the universities outside Oxbridge miscalled redbrick, along with the polytechnics and institutions of management and technology, provided other means of training and entry into the governing élite. And the change in generations was significant, particularly the slow rise to power of those war children, who had suffered the privations of the conflict and of ten years of rationing, and who were not prepared to inflict that experience on their children. That difference of generation – in the opinion of the Oxford historian Hugh Trevor-Roper, now Lord Dacre – provided the real dialectic of historical change. Obsolete ideas such as Communism could be prolonged beyond their natural term, but the discontinuous experience of human generations must carry them away. In his terms, Philby, Burgess and Maclean were already irrelevant, fossils of the past generation to which they had belonged. And as for the band of the Apostles, it was also irrelevant, 'the egregious secret society of self-perpetuating, self-admiring narcissi to which Moore and Forster, Burgess and Blunt belonged. Could it have existed at Oxford? Would it not there have been blown up from within, or laughed out of existence?'

There is an extraordinary tenacity in British clubs and institutions. The Apostles still exist and meet and recruit their embryonic members. They are still influential in the arts and in the government. Following Lord Keynes and Lord Russell, Victor Rothschild entered the House of Lords and became the first head of the Central Policy Review Staff of the Cabinet Office, known as the Think Tank. His directives had a great influence on the policies of some governments. His successor from King's College, Sir Kenneth Berrill, continued the Cambridge and Apostolic tradition of swaying economic policies. Two more Apostles reached the peerage, Noel Annan and Richard Llewelyn-Davies, who had been a Marxist in the thirties at Cambridge. Lord Annan played a great part in the founding and the staffing of the new universities as well as becoming Provost of University College, London, and the Vice-Chancellor of the University of London. His influence on the academic world has been without parallel in his age.

He also influenced the Apostles to change their exclusive ways and elect their first women members. Times were changing, indeed, in the society as in English society. A sign of that change was the speech given by a Canadian Apostle, the economist Professor Harry Johnson, at the society's annual dinner in 1971, welcoming the first Apostolic 'sister'. He actually asked the question of what the Cambridge homosexual tradition had contributed to and subtracted from British public and intellectual life. He praised the work of Lytton Strachey and Maynard Keynes and E.M.Forster, yet warned about their personal and public attacks on orthodoxy that had led to a loss of self-confidence in British society. Perhaps the recent legal recognition of homosexuality by a permissive society had sacrificed the social value of that hidden fringe by making it a legitimate part of the social fabric. Society might turn out to be more tolerant, but less interesting and exciting. The final discrimination that still existed was against women. 'And if ever women achieve equality with men, our culture and society will be a dead duck.'

The old 'culture' of the Apostles was a dying duck. It clung no longer to male bonding or recruitment from one country, one sex, one class, and two Cambridge colleges. It clung only to its unfortunate tradition of secrecy, which its president of 1981, Professor Quentin Skinner, could only justify as an extremely strong convention, accepted by those that joined the society. It was becoming a group open to all the talents and all the 'cultures', welcoming aliens and women, working-class students and scientists, as the top layers of British society were more reluctantly learning to do. Professor Johnson had, indeed, been struck by the supreme arrogance which Keynes had shown in his description of the old Apostolic members at the beginning of the century, 'A small group of gilded youth in Cambridge shielded by inherited social position from the expediencies of the phenomenal world that confronted everyone else, when virtually everyone else was preoccupied with the struggle to stay alive.'

The other 'culture' of C.P.Snow was also a dying duck. It was losing its noble Cavendish tradition of free trade in pure research and of the community of like minds to the necessity of secrecy. Political and military considerations led to the allocation of scientific resources and to restrictions on the spread of information. Where there had been exchange, there was now embargo. Where there had been contact, there was now clandestinity. In a real sense, the physicists of the Cavendish could say, 'We are all Apostles now.'

It is the wrong university tradition. The scientific revolution pioneered at Cambridge was not confined to discoveries in nuclear energy, but included electronics and computers, biochemistry and genetics, crystallography and radio astronomy. The scientists of Cambridge in collaboration, where possible, with the scientists of the world, did change the communications and the perceptions of mankind, and threatened to question and alter the very structure of the human body, of plant and animal life, and perhaps of the universe itself. Restricted from that collaboration by political and strategic rules, their contribution to the flow of human thought must be diminished, perhaps reduced to a backwater of the Cam.

Recently the theoretical physicist Stephen Hawking has overcome the limitations of his physical handicap to probe the black holes and anti-matter of our galaxy. He does not engage in research into star wars and the possible destruction of our planet. There is no limit to the inquiry of the free mind and there should be no limit to the free trade of the fruits of such inquiry outside direct military use. That is the Cambridge tradition that has informed the scholars of the university since its medieval foundation. Its minor tradition of clandestinity and coterie, esoteric research and arcane knowledge, intensity and narcissism only has worth to an establishment which values secret intelligence more than the open exchange of it. That minor tradition, exemplified in the Bloomsbury group and the Apostles and institutionalized in parts of the civil service and of government, derives from an arts 'culture' that cannot and is not changing human society. Science is, within the limits of its funding and its powers.

Notes on Sources

INTRODUCTION TO INTELLIGENCE

For material in this introduction, I am most grateful to:

Miles Copeland, *The Real Spy World* (London, 1974)
Walter A.McDougall, ... *The Heavens and the Earth* (New York, 1985)
Paul Davies, *Superforce: The Search for a Grand Unified Theory of Nature* (New York, 1985)
Heinz R.Pagels, *Perfect Symmetry: The Search for the Beginning of Time* (New York, 1985)
A.Koestler, I. Silone *et alii*, *The God That Failed* R.Crossman ed. (London, 1950)
Solly Zuckerman, *From Apes to Warlords* (London, 1978)
P.G.Wersky, 'British Scientists and "Outsider" Politics, 1931–1945', *Scientific Studies*, 1971, 1
Richard Deacon, *The Cambridge Apostles* (London, 1985)

1 FALLEN LEAVES

Particularly important in the preparation of this chapter were:

Peter Allen, *The Cambridge Apostles: The Early Years* (Cambridge, 1978)
Noel Annan, *The Listener*, 8 February 1951
Noel Annan, '"Our Age": Reflections on Three Generations in England', *Daedalus*, Fall, 1978
Noel Annan, 'Benson's Pleasure', *The London Review of Books*, 4–17 March 1982
Clive Bell, *Old Friends* (London, 1956)
Quentin Bell, *Bloomsbury* (London, 1968)
E.M.Forster, *Goldsworthy Lowes Dickinson* (London, 1934)
R.F.Harrod, *The Prof: A Personal Memoir of Lord Cherwell* (London, 1959)

Michael Holyroyd, *Lytton Strachey: A Critical Biography*, 2 vols (London, 1967–8)

T.E.B.Howarth, *Cambridge Between Two Wars* (London, 1978)

J.K.Johnstone, *The Bloomsbury Group* (London, 1954)

J.M.Keynes, *Essays in Biography* (London, 1933)

J.M.Keynes, *Two Memoirs* (London, 1949)

Paul Levy, *Moore: G.E.Moore and the Cambridge Apostles* (London, 1979)

Desmond MacCarthy, *Portraits* (London, 1931)

Desmond MacCarthy, *Experience* (London, 1935)

S.P.Rosenbaum (ed.), *The Bloomsbury Group* (London, 1975)

The Autobiography of Bertrand Russell, Vol II (London, 1968)

E.Rutherford, 'Obituary of Henry Gwyn Jeffreys Moseley', *Nature*, 96, 1915

Robert Skidelsky, *Oswald Mosley* (London, 1975)

Robert Skidelsky, *John Maynard Keynes: Volume One: Hopes Betrayed, 1883–1920* (London, 1984)

Robert Wohl, *The Generation of 1914* (London, 1980)

Solly Zuckerman, *Scientists and War: The Impact of Science on Military and Civil Affairs* (London, 1966)

2 TWO CULTURES

For material in this chapter, I am also indebted to:

B.V.Babkin, *Pavlov: A Biography* (Chicago, 1951)

Lawrence Badash, *Kapitsa, Rutherford, and the Kremlin* (Santa Barbara, 1985)

Andrew Boyle, *The Climate of Treason: Five Who Spied For Russia* (London, 1979)

J.G.Crowther, *The Cavendish Laboratory, 1874–1974* (London, 1974)

Richard Deacon, *The British Connection* (1979, unpublished)

Robert Graves and Alan Hodge, *The Long Weekend: A Social History of Great Britain, 1918–1939* (London, 1940)

P.L.Kapitsa, 'Recollections of Lord Rutherford', *Proceedings of the Royal Society*, 1966

Kay MacLeod, *Politics, Professionalisation and the Organisation of Scientists: the Association of Scientific Workers, 1917–42* (Thesis, University of Sussex, 1975, unpublished)

F.S.Northedge and Audrey Wells, *Britain and Soviet Communism: The Impact of a Revolution* (London, 1982)

Albert Parry (ed.), *Peter Kapitsa on Life and Science* (New York, 1968)

Mark Popovsky, *Science in Chains* (London, 1980)
Anthony Powell, *Messengers of Day* (London, 1978)
Rutherford Papers, Cambridge University Library
C.P.Snow, *Variety of Men* (London, 1967)
C.P.Snow, *The Physicists* (London, 1981)

3 CLIMACTERIC

The following books and articles have also been of great service to me in this chapter:

Noel Annan, *Roxburgh of Stowe* (London, 1970)
Alan Bennett, *The South Bank Show*, 7 October 1984
Percy Cradock, *Recollections of the Cambridge Union, 1815–1939* (Cambridge, 1953)
Harriette Flory, 'The Arcos Raid and the Rupture of Anglo–Soviet Relations, 1927', *Journal of Contemporary History*, Vol 12, No. 4, October 1977
Andrew Hodges, *Alan Turing: The Enigma* (New York, 1984)
C.Day Lewis, *The Mind in Chains* (London, 1937)
George Steiner, 'The Cleric of Treason', *New Yorker*, 8 December 1980
Michael Straight, *After Long Silence* (London, 1983)

4 AN EXCESS OF GENEROSITY

For this chapter, I am particularly indebted to:

Cambridge University Studies (Cambridge, 1933)
T.E.B.Howarth, *Cambridge Between the Wars*, op. cit. ch. 1
Julian Huxley, *Memories* (London, 1970)

5 THE MOLES AND THE TROJAN HORSE

In addition to the works cited previously, I am particularly indebted to:

Bill Alexander, *British Volunteers for Liberty: Spain, 1936–1939* (London, 1982)
P.M.S.Blackett, *Studies of War: Nuclear and Conventional* (Edinburgh, 1962)
Christopher Caudwell, *The Crisis in Physics* (London, 1938)
Robert Cecil, 'The Cambridge Comintern', *The Missing Dimension: Governments and Intelligence Communities in the Twentieth Century*, C.Andrew and D.Dilks (eds.) (London, 1984)

Ronald Clark, *J.B.S.: The Life and Work of J.B.S.Haldane* (London, 1968)
Claud Cockburn, *In Time of Trouble* (London, 1956)
Patricia Cockburn, *The Years of THE WEEK* (London, 1968)
J.G.Crowther, *British Scientists of the Twentieth Century* (London, 1952)
Tom Driberg, *Guy Burgess: A Portrait with Background* (London, 1956)
G.Hartcup and T.E.Allibone, *Cockcroft and the Atom* (Bristol, 1984)
Herbert L.Matthews, *Half of Spain Died* (New York, 1973)
Jessica Mitford, *Hons and Rebels* (London, 1977)
George Orwell, *The Collected Essays*, 'An Age Like This, 1920–1940', Vol
  1 (London, 1968)
Anthony Purdy and Douglas Sutherland, *Burgess and Maclean* (London,
  1963)
Goronwy Rees, *A Bundle of Sensations* (London, 1960)
Goronwy Rees, *A Chapter of Accidents* (London, 1972)
Sir Stephen Runciman to Richard Deacon in *The Cambridge Apostles*
  (London, 1985)
Stuart Samuels, 'The Left Book Club', *Journal of Contemporary History*, Vol
  1, No. 2, 1966
C.P.Snow, 'The Moral Un-Neutrality of Science' (1960), *Public Affairs*
  (London, 1971)
Hugh Thomas, *The Spanish Civil War* (London, 1961)
Philip Toynbee, *Friends Apart* (London, 1954)
Nigel West, *MI5: British Security Service Operations 1909–1945* (London,
  1981)
Solly Zuckerman, *Scientists and War: The Impact of Science on Military and
  Civil Affairs* (London, 1966)

6 THE CRISIS OF COMMITMENT

In addition to the books and articles quoted in previous chapters, I am
particularly indebted to conversations with the late Dennis Brogan and
to:

Bill Alexander, *British Volunteers for Liberty: Spain 1936–1939* (London,
  1982)
David Childs, 'The British Communist Party and the War, 1939–41: Old
  Slogans Revived', *Journal of Contemporary History*, Vol 12, No. 2, 1977
1939: The Communist Party of Great Britain and the War, John Attfield and
  Stephen Williams (eds) (London, 1984)
Cyril Connolly, *The Missing Diplomats* (London, 1952)
Alexander Foote, *Handbook for Spies* (London, 1949)

Douglas Hyde, *I Believed* (London, 1952)

John Langdon-Davies, *Finland: the First Total War* (London, 1940)

John Lehmann, *In My Own Time: Memoirs of a Literary Life* (Boston, 1969)

James Leutze, 'The Secret of the Churchill–Roosevelt Correspondence: September 1939 – May 1940', *Journal of Contemporary History*, Vol 10, No. 3, 1975

Robert Manne, 'The British Decision for Alliance with Russia, May 1939', *Journal of Contemporary History*, Vol 9, No. 3, 1974

Edward Marsh, *Ambrosia and Small Beer: A Correspondence with Christopher Hassall* (London, 1964)

Malcolm Muggeridge, *The Infernal Grove* (London, 1973)

Michael Straight, *After Long Silence* (London, 1983)

7 SECURITY RISK

I am also indebted to a conversation with Fred Warner and to these additional sources:

J.D.Bernal, *The Social Function of Science* (London, 1940)

Andrew Boyle, *The Chariots of Treason* (London, 1979)

Cyril Connolly, *The Missing Diplomats* (London, 1952)

David J.Dalbin, *Soviet Espionage* (New Haven, 1956)

Tom Driberg, *Ruling Passions* (London, 1977)

Richard Hirsch, *The Soviet Spies* (London, 1947)

H.Montgomery Hyde, *The Atom Bomb Spies* (London, 1980)

A.Koestler, I.Silone, *et alii*, *The God That Failed* R.Crossman (ed.) (London, 1950)

B.Page, D.Leitch, P.Knightley, *Philby: The Spy Who Betrayed a Generation* (London, 1968)

Kim Philby, *My Secret War* (London, 1968)

Chapman Pincher, *Too Secret Too Long* (London, 1984)

Lord Rothschild, *Random Variables* (London, 1984)

Ronald Seth, *Forty Years of Soviet Spying* (London, 1952)

Stephen Spender, *Journals* (London, 1985)

H.Trevor-Roper, *The Philby Affair: Espionage, Treason, and Secret Services* (London, 1968)

Solly Zuckerman, *From Apes to Warlords* (London, 1978)

8 CONSCIENTIOUS FISSION

Of particular interest in the preparation of this chapter were:

The Cockcroft papers in the Churchill College Archive, particularly
Wilson Carroll to Guy Hartup, 1 September 1980

Noel Annan, "Our Age", op. cit. ch. 1
A.M.Biew, *Kapitsa*, op. cit. ch. 2
S.D.Drell, *Science*, 2 August 1968
J.Kugelmass and J.Goulden, 'The double cross that gave the reds the
    H-BOMB', *Look*, 13 July 1954
James Lees-Milne, *Harold Nicolson: A Biography* (2 vols, London, 1984)
David E.Lilienthal, *Journals: The Atomic Energy Years 1945–50* (Vol II, New
    York, 1964)
Henry Pelling, *The Labour Governments, 1945–51* (London, 1984)
Anthony Powell, *Messengers of Day*, op. cit. ch. 2
Strobe Talbott (ed.), *Khushchev Remembers: The Last Testament* (New York,
    1976)
D.ter Haar (ed.), *The Collected Papers of P.I.Kapitsa*, 3 vols (Oxford, 1967)
Ann Thwaite and Ronald Hayman (eds.), *My Oxford, My Cambridge*
    (London, 1977)
H.York, *The Advisors: Oppenheimer, Teller and the Superbomb* (San Francisco,
    1976)

9 A CHANGING OF THE GUARD

For the material in this chapter, I am indebted to:

Tom Driberg, *Guy Burgess*, op. cit. ch. 5
Harry Longmuir interviewing Sir Dennis Proctor, *Daily Mail*, 9 November
    1981
The Observer, 24 March 1985, 'Revealed at Last: The Deadly Secrets of
    Britain's A-bombs.'
George Steiner, 'The Cleric of Treason', op. cit. ch. 3
James D.Watson, *The Double Helix* (London, 1968)
Andrew Wilson, 'Acts of the Apostles', *The Observer*, 8 November 1981
Solly Zuckerman, *From Apes to Warlords*, op. cit. ch. 7

10 O YES - MY COUNTRY, WHITE AND WRONG

For material in this chapter, I am indebted to interviews with James
Cornford, Margaret Drabble, Alun Williams, Anthony Howard, and
material from these published works:

Vernon Bogdanor and Robert Skidelsky (eds.), *The Age of Affluence, 1951–1964* (London, 1970)

Christopher Booker, *The Neophiliacs* (London, 1969)

John Gross, *Times Literary Supplement*, May 1974

B.S. Johnson (ed.), *All Bull: The National Servicemen* (London, 1973)

F.R. Leavis and Michael Yudkin, *Two Cultures? The Significance of C.P. Snow* (London, 1962)

Walter H. McDougall, ... *The Heavens and the Earth*, op. cit. Introduction

Peter Medawar, *The Limits of Science* (Oxford, 1985)

C.P. Snow, *The Two Cultures: and a Second Look* (Cambridge, 1964)

Ann Thwaite and Ronald Hayman (eds.), *My Oxford, My Cambridge*, op. cit. ch. 8

Raymond Williams, 'Gravity's Python', *The London Review of Books*, 4–17 December 1980

Roger Wilmut, *From Fringe to Flying Circus* (London, 1980)

11 JUST TO BE ON THE SAFE SIDE

For material in this final chapter, I am grateful to:

G.T. Allison, A. Carnesale, and J.S. Nye, Jr. (eds.), *Hawks, Doves, and Owls: An Agenda for Avoiding Nuclear War* (New York, 1985)

David Caute, *The Fellow-Travellers* (London, 1973)

L.L. Greenberg, 'Policy-making in the USSR Academy of Sciences', *Journal of Contemporary History*, October 1973

P.L. Kapitsa, 'Recollections of Lord Rutherford', *Proceedings of the Royal Society*, 1966

Walter Laqueur, *A World of Secrets: The Uses and Limits of Intelligence* (New York, 1984)

Walter Laqueur, *International Herald Tribune*, 5–6 October 1985

Gene Lyons, 'Athens Versus Sparta', *Newsweek*, April 1985

Hugh Trevor-Roper, *The Philby Affair*, op. city. ch. 7

Hugh Trevor-Roper, 'Acts of the Apostles', *New York Review of Books*, 31 March 1983

Solly Zuckerman, 'The Prospects for Nuclear War', *New York Review of Books*, 15 August 1985

Index